LEAD

LEAD

GARY BURNISON

WILEY

To my esteemed colleagues.

CONTENTS

THE ABSOLUTES FOR LEADERS

As a coach for my son's basketball team, at the end of every practice I ask a player to attempt a three-point shot. If the player makes the shot, the team gets excused from the last drill of running laps. Last season, we had a great team. There was one player, however, who was a little shorter, a little smaller, and not as athletic as the rest. In fact, this boy, Jason, hadn't scored a single basket all year. But, unlike the others, he had never missed a single practice. ⇒

On the final practice before the championship game, I asked the team, "Who wants to take the three-point shot?" Nine pleading hands flew up; one hand did not—Jason's. Something compelled me to give him the ball as the others grumbled about the laps they were sure they'd be running.

When Jason shot the ball, it hit the back of the rim, bounced high off the iron, and grazed the basket on the way down, unsuccessfully. Immediately I did something I had never done before: I gave him the ball again. Jason didn't hesitate and the entire team watched as the ball swished through the net. Jason's grin was a mile wide as the other kids jumped up and down in celebration. Out of the corner of my eye, I caught a glimpse of Jason's dad with a

Leadership is making others believe, turning vision into reality.

satisfied smile. Later, he said to me in a voice choked with emotion, "I don't care if Jason scores any points on Sunday, that made the entire season for me."

We did win the championship, but frankly I don't remember the final score or how we did it. All I remember was the beaming smile of a 12-year-old boy and the wet eyes of his father.

Leadership is making others believe—in themselves, in the organization, in the impossible—then, translating that belief into reality.

Leadership requires you to forget all the lauded, impressive qualities that helped you climb the ladder and to shift your focus outward; your measure of success will be in what others achieve. Easy to intellectualize, but elusive to actualize, leadership is part strategy, but mostly judgment. It's sense, and sensibility.

Fortunately, there are certain fundamental elements to guide you, elements that are as critical in today's hyper-connected technosphere as they were in the days when contracts were written on the skins of animals.

This book is a compass for discovering these absolutes. Every organization starts with a vision and a PURPOSE—the "what" and the "why" of its existence. Then comes STRATEGY, the "how" and, more subtly, the "when" of its game plan to realize that purpose. PEOPLE are truly the essential element, embracing the purpose and executing the strategy. MEASURE minds the organization's progress—what is working and what is not.

EMPOWER means to delegate to people, not just as individual performers, but as teams aligned with purpose and strategy. When success arrives, keep people motivated with REWARD—a celebration of who they are, not just compensation for what they've done.

Next are the Absolutes that define the activities in which you, as the leader, must constantly engage. They are ANTICIPATE, to make calculated bets about tomorrow; NAVIGATE, to adjust and correct your course in real time; COMMUNICATE, to connect emotionally with others; LISTEN, to welcome the truth and gain trust; and LEARN, which must be a lifelong passion for every leader—all of which culminates with LEAD.

Leadership can be learned and absorbed only by doing, starting with the most important lesson of all: To lead others, you must first lead yourself. May you find in these pages both information and inspiration as you define your leadership path—a journey that, ultimately, is about empowering others.

GARY BURNISON
CEO, *Korn/Ferry International*

LEAD

"THE change you

want to see in the world

starts with you."

1

LEAD

Remember the thrilling rush of freedom, the motivating jolt of pride, the first time you pedaled all alone on a two-wheeled bike? As you propelled yourself forward in that glorious moment there was, for most of us, someone looking on that made it possible. In their seemingly modest actions can be found the DNA of powerful leadership: a mode of being that is less about analytics and decision-making, and much more about aligning, motivating, and empowering others. ⇒

Your people drive financial performance: Who's on the bikes and how they feel is more important than where those bikes are going. The nearly irrefutable lesson gleaned from over a century of management theory and practice—a message reinforced by endless data and anecdotes from the great business gurus like Tom Peters and Jim Collins—is that great companies that get the people part right tend to get everything else right, too.

Fact is, we hyper-focus on numbers because numbers are, in a word, easy. They follow rules; they can be manipulated at will. People, well, not so much.

So here's the question. How do you get your people pedaling with that freedom and pride?

How do you get the people part right?

There's a story about Gandhi, perhaps apocryphal but widely told. A mother brought her young son before the Mahatma to ask him to help cure him of his obsession with sugar. Gandhi said, "Bring your boy back in a week, and then I will speak to him."

A week later the mother returned with her son, and Gandhi told the boy, "Stop eating sweets. They are not good for you." Realizing that was *it*, that was all the great leader was going to say, the mother was understandably confused.

"You could have told him that last week—why did you have us come back?" she asked.

"Last week," Gandhi replied, "I, too, was eating a great deal of sugar." Moral of the story: The change you want to see in the world starts with you.

Leadership is grace and restraint.

The line between confidence and cockiness is humbleness.

Spirited e-mails filled with bold announcements, rah-rah company retreats, or enlightened HR policies and the like are all meaningless abstractions unless they're grounded in the everyday concrete example you, as leader, set for the organization. Gandhi may have introduced us to this model of the humble leader leading by example, but it's been validated more recently by the capitalist gurus found at the corporate ashram we know today as IBM.

A few years back, IBM researchers huddled up to identify the traits of their most high-impact employees. What they found was that ambition alone was only mediocre; ambition plus *intellectual humility* was the winning combination. They dubbed this trait *humbition*. Summed up by William Taylor, the co-founder of *Fast Company* magazine and the author of *Practically Radical*, "They understood that if you want to have an impact today, your job is no longer to be the smartest person in the room, and your job is not to solve every problem and identify every opportunity. Your job is to ask yourself: What does it mean to be an impact player in a world where nobody alone is as smart as everybody together?"

Balance heroics with humility.

In other words, great leaders must be constantly ready to find their next best ideas in the mouths of their most junior employee. Being a leader isn't about enforcement, but empowerment—which means being **all in, all the time,** living and breathing the success of the organization. Being "the change you want," with employees, and with customers, too.

When people hit the top of the corporate pyramid, they can start to feel isolated, a cohort of one sitting on a very sharp point. And then another pyramid appears, inverted and pointed down at them, filled with layer upon layer of constituencies: media, stockholders, analysts, unions. . . .

To avoid being speared, you must focus your best energy on the only two groups that have more power than you to make your company successful: your customers and your employees. Everything else is a distraction.

As the leader of an organization, therefore, you must maintain two perspectives. One is "outside in," understanding how your customers perceive and interact with your organization. The other is "inside out," constantly putting yourself in your employees' shoes. Do they feel cared for? Do they have ample opportunity to grow? Do they know they matter? It's your job to tell them, again and again, by building a culture that constantly celebrates their efforts.

Leadership also requires you to find the careful balance between two faces: your authentic humanity, with all its fickle rhythms and unvarnished blemishes, and your symbolic role as the head of the

Words motivate,
actions inspire.

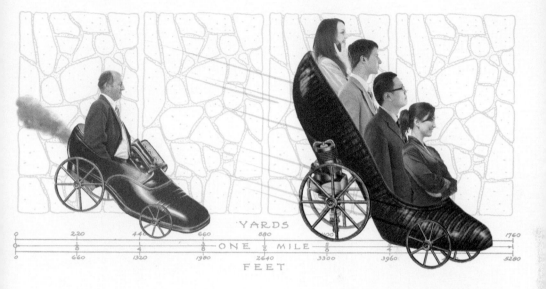

organization. Although your focus is always on the people—the in-dividuals—on your team, in *their* eyes you are at times a function, and not a person. Having a "gray day" doesn't relinquish your re-sponsibility to set the team's reality. People must be able to look in your eyes and feel in their bellies, "We *will* make it together."

Which brings us back to Gandhi and humbition. Leadership requires a unique ability to balance confidence, restraint, and au-thenticity with the humility and good sense to rise above "me" to

Your road is the "high road"—always, with no exceptions.

embrace "we." Paul "Bear" Bryant, the legendary University of Alabama football coach, got it perfectly when he said, "If anything goes bad, I did it. If anything goes semi-good, we did it. If anything goes really good, then you did it. That's all it takes to get people to win football games for you." And, it can be said, to get people to win at the game of business.

True leadership isn't heroism. Heroism is episodic, while leadership is *systemic*, defined by a hundred things, big and small, mostly sacrifices, done every day with consistency and sincerity. It's not your job to be a hero, but instead to help create and celebrate them. ✳

To lead others, you must first lead yourself.

THINGS TO LISTEN FOR

WHEN LEAD IS IN PLACE . . .	WHEN THERE IS A NEED FOR LEAD . . .
"I recognize how fortunate I am to have this opportunity."	"Without me, this would have been a disaster."
"We are going to figure this out."	"Why we're doing this is not important, just get it done."
"How can we turn this crisis into an opportunity?"	"Who is responsible for this?"

IDEAS FOR ACTION

Do

Humility as an Anchor

CULTIVATE HUMILITY The fresh air at and near the top of the corporate ladder smells fine. It is also the perfect microclimate to breed arrogance. You are, after all, an extremely capable person. So few have done what you've done. You've developed many skills through many experiences. Some people might even say you are wise.

All might be true—and yet, you need to find a way to cultivate humility. Too much self-confidence narrows your peripheral vision. Leading your organization as though you've got it all figured out makes you and your company a target for negative surprises. Humility keeps you aware, alert, and nimble.

Consciously cultivate curiosity, ask good questions, and listen to new and possibly unconventional ideas that keep your business healthy. Create a rolling schedule of novel experiences and opportunities to learn so that you can easily slip into your "beginner" suit. Get out of your office, often. And embrace these powerful phrases: *I don't know. Help me understand. You're right!*

DEMONSTRATE GRACE AND PATIENCE In some circles, impatience is considered a virtue. It's mistakenly equated with being results-driven. In some rare instances when deadlines continually get missed, results aren't there, or standards are slack, then absolutely a show of hot-tempered disappointment is appropriate.

But let's be very clear: Impatience doesn't inspire high performance, it inspires fear, which can be as debilitating to your team's critical thinking and engagement as alcohol or drugs.

Recall what happened inside the cockpit of Air France Flight 447 before it crashed into the Atlantic Ocean in 2009: Its pilot, terrified and inexperienced, kept pulling back the stick, despite the fact that it was clearly leading them into a steep descent. *Popular Mechanics* called his actions irrational but not inexplicable, explaining, "Intense psychological stress tends to shut down the part of the brain responsible for innovative, creative thought. Instead, we tend to revert to the familiar and the well-rehearsed." In other words, the pilot defaulted to the maneuvers he knew best, those performed at low altitude. There, pulling back the stick would have saved them, instead of crashing them into the fathoms.

So, ease up on the stick. Embrace the oxymoronic motto of Emperor Augustus and "make haste slowly" (*festina lente*). Grace under pressure and patience flow from humility, and are what turn crisis into opportunity.

REMEMBER YOUR "WHY" Keep things in perspective. Why are you in the position you are in? What is your purpose? Put business results and bonuses aside, and consider your leadership legacy. How are you changing each and every life your leadership touches? Staying grounded in a broader sense of purpose can produce a ripple effect of positive change in people—change that may not fit neatly into a strategy deck but helps meet business goals in surprising and intangible ways.

If you have no clear definition of your greater purpose, how do you know what you're really looking to achieve? How do you know whether you're winning or losing? For that matter, how do you know why you're putting in those 14-hour days in the first place?

When you can answer the "why" of your work with a clear, crisp answer that comes equally from your head and your heart, almost inevitably there is a shift from focusing on the short-term bottom line to the long-term goal; from errors to opportunities; from imposing control to instilling confidence.

Shifting from "I" to "We"

LEAD IN SERVICE TO OTHERS As a leader it can be tempting to make it about you. Your team is orbiting around you, the sun. In the dry wit of the 1920s classic, *Wisdom in Small Doses*, "It is well to remember that the entire universe, with one trifling exception, is composed of others." At the end of the day, it is not about you. It's about the business, it's about the customers, it's about your employees. You are responsible for so many people's welfare. That is the weight of the position you hold.

BE A STEWARD OF THE ORGANIZATION Your role as leader of an organization is not permanent. Think of yourself less as a life-appointed Supreme Court Justice—beholden to no one, swayed by nothing—and more as the President trying to have as impactful a four-year term as possible on the constituencies you were elected to represent. If every day you work to make the lives of your employees and customers better, there's a good chance you'll last longer than the five years that is the average tenure of a CEO.

TAKE ACCOUNTABILITY   Share the credit, accept the blame. Being a leader is different from being a hero. A hero gets to come in and save the day and bask in the accolades during the victory parade. Not so for a leader. A leader's work is about empowering other people to step up and take responsibility and then catching them when they fall, all the while maintaining that you are accountable for the success or failure of the entire business. The biggest obstacle to teams reaching their fullest potential is an absence of accountability. Display a standard for it at the very top—rigorously, consistently, and publicly—and all the teams in your organization will follow suit. It's not easy, but that's the job.

Being All in, All the Time

WATCH YOUR MOODS   You aren't just anybody; you are the boss. Employees are scrutinizing your tone of voice, facial expressions, body language, and demeanor, constantly looking to decipher whatever it is they think you're not saying. Sharpen your self-awareness and exude stability so that people won't be distracted by small dips in your emotional trend line, or project their anxieties onto your haphazard squint.

Regardless, you will have some bad days, experience stress, and need to vent. Find a safe person to confide in—it could be your spouse, an executive coach, or a mentor. When you know you have a place to take your concerns and discuss them openly, you'll find it easier to maintain your Lincoln-like composure throughout the rest of the day.

STAY PRESENT Rushing from one meeting to the next. Ruminating over concerns about future projections. Having to multi-task and shift gears quickly. All of these things contribute to mental exhaustion and distraction. Do what you can to stay focused and present. Protect time on your calendar for necessary reflection. Find rituals that help you prepare for your day and wrap it up. The more you can minimize the scattered feeling, the more people will perceive that you are present and attentive to the issue at hand.

KEEP YOUR WORDS AND ACTIONS CONSISTENT Your integrity is paramount. It's a threshold requirement for the position you hold. A lot rides on whether people believe that they can trust you. Studies show that employees who trust their senior leaders are more engaged at work. Think about how the performance of the entire organization can be influenced by your integrity. Do what's right. Say what you mean. Keep your word. If you can't keep your word, make amendments to your word and acknowledge the change. Take responsibility. Share the right information with the right people. Put the well-being of your employees, customers, and the organization first. ■

> "It is well to remember
> that the entire universe,
> with one trifling exception,
> is composed of others."
>
> JOHN ANDREW HOLMES, *Wisdom in Small Doses*

Questions for reflection . . .

How do I maintain composure under stress?

Do I share credit but take the blame?

Am I more focused on image or results?

How do I stay in touch with the business and our customers?

What do I do every day that inspires and motivates others?

In what situations am I more likely to react versus respond?

"PURPOSE,

resolution, and harmony unify life and give it meaning by transforming it into a seamless flow experience."

MIHALY CSIKSZENTMIHALYI
Flow: The Psychology of Optimal Experience

THE SECOND
ABSOLUTE
FOR LEADERS: PUR

POSE

It was a bleak, increasingly scary time in the last months of 1942, as the daily news was filled with reports about the air, sea, and land battles of World War II. Unbeknownst to nearly anyone, President Franklin D. Roosevelt was busy hatching a top-secret plan. The mission: harness nuclear energy to build a weapon powerful enough to decisively end World War II. ⇒

Spanning four years, involving 130,000 workers and 6,000 scientists, The Manhattan Project was an unprecedented scientific endeavor with unthinkably tight deadlines and quite literally the fate of the world hanging in the balance. Whether you regard it as travesty or a triumph, the creation of the atomic bomb was, in terms of leadership and organization, a historic achievement. Few are aware, however, of the project's lackluster early beginnings.

Purpose is the anchor of the organization.

In a desire for complete secrecy, the U.S. government told the scientists that their work was in the service of "classified war work." The scientists plodded along with all the genius of an eighth-grade remedial science class. Finally, project managers decided to tell them exactly what they were working for: ending the war. Everything changed: chalk flew. Lights stayed on late into the night. Ideas fired like rockets. And the rest is history.

Few of us will ever play a game with such stakes, thankfully, and yet the job of a leader is to identify, communicate, and embody stakes that truly matter to every constituency inside and outside of your company. Large or small, Fortune 500 or community group, every great organization is established for a reason that goes beyond profit. Leadership begins with that purpose—the "why" of the organization.

Certainly, your people are working for their own self-interest; that's why you pay them. Handsome salaries get the job done, but rarely do they get it done with speed, excellence, ingenuity, and care. People long for meaning in their lives, and so must the organization.

Understanding the *why* behind what we're doing lets us connect our individual actions to a larger, deeper purpose. Knowing that purpose can make careers, make companies, or make history. It can even transform the absurdities or even indignities of daily life—our congested commute, the tightness of a necktie, the endless movement of our fingers across a keyboard—into *meaningful, impactful actions.*

Purpose must be omnipresent—on the walls and in the halls.

"To make all athletes better
through passion, science,
and the relentless pursuit
of innovation."

Mission Statement, Under Armour

**Purpose must have a long shadow
over the organization.**

Hungarian psychologist Mihaly Csikszentmihalyi put it beautifully in his book *Flow: The Psychology of Optimal Experience:* "Purpose, resolution, and harmony unify life and give it meaning by transforming it into a seamless flow experience. . . . Every living moment will make sense, and most of it will be enjoyable." Purpose is the organization's soul, allowing self-interest to become shared interest, convincing employees their efforts are making a difference in some wider, more important context.

But how to make that purpose tangible? It doesn't just "happen." *Everyone at every level of the organization* needs to understand in their gut *why* they are working together and the vision—a clear picture of what the company will look like when your purpose is realized. Your job as a leader is to paint that destination, graffiti-like, over everything your people do—and perhaps even more importantly, to find a way to delegate that responsibility to others.

Consider former Charles Schwab CEO David Pottruck. Though his tenure didn't survive the company's post-dotcom-crash low, he is widely credited with transforming that company's culture by aligning employees around the belief that they weren't money managers. They were, rather, the *custodians of their client's dreams.* As he described it in his book *Clicks and Mortar,* "Around here we think we're curing cancer." (It's worth noting, too, that Pottruck didn't come into Charles Schwab a natural leader; he worked at it for years with Terry Pearce, the executive coach who would become his co-author, and by all accounts transformed himself and his leadership capabilities.)

Purpose is the bridge from "what we've been" to "what we will be."

To achieve true alignment around a purpose and vision, you need scale, and to create scale, you need to be able to delegate purpose-driven decision-making. Don't make the mistake of hoarding meaning because you think it elevates you. Spread it around and watch your own value, and your company's, rise.

Back to Charles Schwab. The company's founder and namesake had his own role in building the company's celebrated culture, to be sure, but it was Pottruck who was truly able to *operationalize purpose*, to delegate the message so that hundreds of people could make thousands of decisions that were directionally in line with his intent. Pottruck would never have established himself as a great leader if he had made himself the only dream-catcher.

Purpose is never about the leader, but it does start with the leader. Whether you are a CEO of a global company or the head of the local PTA, you must embody the purpose of the organization. People need to look at you and viscerally connect to the truth of that purpose—in your eyes, actions, and words. ✳

THINGS TO LISTEN FOR

WHEN PURPOSE IS IN PLACE . . .

"I understand how the work I do fits into the bigger picture."

"I know exactly why I am here and the role I play."

"We don't make widgets. We improve lives."

WHEN THERE IS A NEED FOR PURPOSE . . .

"I feel like there is a lack of coordination here—we're all off working on our own projects."

"It's hard to know how my success will be measured; the goal seems to change so frequently."

"This organization lacks clear direction, which leaves us in disconnected silos without a common goal."

IDEAS FOR ACTION

Do

Getting Purpose

CREATE A TEAM CHARTER A charter articulates the vision, crystallizing an organization's purpose for those inside and outside the organization. The best charters answer the questions: *Who are we? Why are we here? What is our unique contribution to the larger vision?* A charter may stand for many years or it may get revised and touched up each quarter. Either way, it is a touchstone for people to better understand the team's focus and how it serves both internal and external customers. It's also an essential leadership and decision-making tool for you and your delegates. In the words of Jim Collins, "The rare ability to balance continuity and change—requiring a consciously practiced discipline—is closely linked to the ability to develop a vision. Vision provides guidance about what to preserve and what to change."

KNOW YOUR PLACE IN THE WORLD While it might be aspirational, have a clear idea of the place the organization holds in the world. Think about Southwest Airlines: Everyone knows that they're democratizing the skies, making travel affordable and convenient—an idea that motivates employees as much as it drives revenue. Such a well-defined brand proposition doesn't happen without design and delivery. What do you want to be known for? What associations do you want people to have with your brand? What are the differentiating characteristics of your organization or team that make you stand out? How does that define and refine your purpose?

DISCOVER YOUR UNIQUE CONTRIBUTION Reflect on where the company's greatest strength meets the world's greatest need. Companies that veer too far from their core competences tend to lose focus and struggle to compete. Figure out what you can be best at. Focus on what you're doing that no one else is doing. That will help shape the purpose and direction for your organization.

Communicating Purpose

UNDERSTAND YOUR AUDIENCE In order to effectively communicate an established purpose and vision, you need to understand *who* you are talking to and how they fit into the bigger picture. Get to know different constituencies and become aware of their vantage point. What work do they do? How do they add value? How do they see themselves in the context of the whole? You need to meet your audience where they sit before you get them to entertain your broader vision and purpose.

PUSH THE RIGHT BUTTONS Different people are motivated by different things. We all come to work for different reasons and want to contribute in different ways. One person may feel strongly about social responsibility, another is energized by innovation. Assess what matters most to people and link what they value most to what is constant, the vision and purpose of the organization. Translating the vision this way motivates, engages, and empowers your people to work for their most compelling self-interests.

BE AUTHENTIC AND SHOW YOUR COMMITMENT Trust in senior leadership is a much scarcer commodity these days than a decade ago, and yet it hugely affects workforce engagement—in one study having *double* the impact of trust in immediate managers. For better or worse, employees are going to sense from a mile away whether or not you, the leader, are passionate and committed to the purpose you are touting. Earn their trust by being consistent, on message, transparent, and *authentic*. Nothing is more important than your authenticity. Until you have tapped into who you are, what motivates you, and why you believe in the future direction of the company, employees will sniff out false leadership and turn their attention to something that really matters.

Aligning Purpose

BE RELENTLESSLY CLEAR Never make assumptions about what people know or don't know. Find ways to communicate the purpose and vision directly. Do teams have monthly meetings you can attend in person? How about setting up town halls? Overcommunication is key in getting the message across; the rule of thumb in marketing is that people need to touch your brand three times before they even remember you exist.

Listening is equally important. Make sure to leave time for questions. It speaks to your investment in their understanding, and gives people time to process and co-create the answer to how their work fits into the company's purpose.

CASCADE PURPOSE THROUGHOUT THE ORGANIZA-TION Once you've engaged your leadership team on the purpose and vision for the future, make sure that they have the tools to talk to their teams. Maybe you provide them with talking points or frequently asked questions. The opportunity to deliver the message directly to their teams fosters a sense of ownership. Find ways to let the company's purpose become everyone's purpose—the only smart, scalable model for leadership.

MAKE IT TANGIBLE FOR THE TEAM Once the purpose is communicated, it's important to provide concrete examples of how that purpose comes to life on a daily basis. What changes now that the purpose is defined? Help your leaders set expectations for their teams. Be specific about the goals and tactics that need to be carried out. And, be clear about a timeframe. Without these concrete directions and expectations, the purpose may never fully come to life in the organization. "He who has a why to live can bear with almost any how" (Nietzche) will come to pass—but only if you can be successful in making the *why* real. ∎

Questions for reflection . . .

Why am I here?

Why does this
company exist?

What is the one
thing this organization
can be best at?

How do our strengths
meet the needs of
our customers?

What gets me out of bed
in the morning?

How would I articulate
why we do what we do?

"YOU only find oil

if you drill wells.
You may think you're
finding it when you're
drawing maps and
studying logs,
but you have to drill."

JOHN MASTERS, *The Hunters*

3

STRA

Kodak Film, the iconic American company to-day mired in bankruptcy, is popularly believed to have been completely broadsided by digital technology—but that's not exactly accurate. In fact, they invented the world's first digital camera in the effectively prehistoric era of 1978. The trouble was, because they considered themselves a *film* company, they threw it (and their lead in the digital space) in a broom closet. In the years that followed, Kodak focused on its purpose—to help customers capture and share their most treasured memories. But, they stuck with a strategy that hadn't failed them yet—film. ⇒

TEGY

And so it is that technology didn't kill Kodak; lack of strategy did. No company, including yours, is immune, and to do it right in this era requires a dramatically more fluid approach than it did in the past.

Strategy was never truly linear, but you used to be able to get away with treating it that way. Today's strategic thinking must be dynamic and perpetual. With purpose as your constant guide, a strategic planner always needs to have not just his ear, but many ears, to the ground.

To visualize this new distributed model, look no further than the good old NFL. Management expert Steve Tobak has pointed out that so-called "audibles," when a quarterback changes the play from the scrimmage line, were once far and few between. Strategy was delivered in the huddle. Today, an increasingly sophisticated game now relies on these last-minute pivots called out by the quarterback.

It's up to you to find and coach your quarterbacks, and be constantly in communication, so that the game plan, however fluid in time and space, remains clear to the rest of the organization; everyone at every moment needs to know the difference between truly important and merely urgent.

It's equally your job to make sure the strategy stays aligned to the common purpose, the "why." It's important for the overall health of the company, but it's also key to helping prepare your people for change. That "why" helps you bend time and space so that they can see how an apparent detour actually moves them forward.

> **Strategy is not just direction;
> it's velocity.**

That's important, because here's the humbling truth: Your people won't move faster than they can handle, and no strategy is any good if you can't execute it on schedule. Even the most brilliant plan is a failed plan if you can only get halfway there. As John Masters, the Canadian oil and gas wildcatter, wrote in *The Hunters*, ". . . it is amazing how few oil people really understand that you only find oil if you drill wells. You may think you're finding it when you're drawing maps and studying logs, but you have to drill."

In other words, strategic velocity is as important as strategic direction, and the finesse of leadership is to shift the culture at a pace that matches your execution timeline. That means setting aside time—the huddle—for communicating strategy, so that people

**90 percent of strategy is execution
and 90 percent of execution is people.**

fully understand the "how" and can fill in the "how to" with their on-the-ground knowledge, but it also means giving people tools for game-time changeups. You can't possibly predict and account for all the ways any given strategy will drive daily decision-making across a range of functions from the bottom to the top of the organization. But you *can* empower people with knowledge to make the right decisions and redirect their energy and their actions to align with this new game.

**Focus on the "how,"
not the "how to."**

> ## "The limiting factor in our ability to build strong organizations is just humans' ability to all get on the same page and go in the same direction."
>
> SALLY BLOUNT
> *Dean, Kellogg School of Management, Northwestern University*

Most leaders focus themselves too much on the plan and forget the people, so that's what we've emphasized here—sharpening your ability to make your leadership participatory. But there will also be times when you need the confidence to make decisions—to drive rather than build consensus in moments of uncertainty.

There's a bluff in Montana at the confluence of the Marias and Missouri Rivers that is today known as Decision Point Overlook. In 1805, Meriwether Lewis climbed it, trying to find a vantage point to

Differentiate between the important and the urgent. Devote yourself to the important; delegate the urgent.

tell him which of these two forks was the true Missouri, which he believed would be his channel to the Columbia River. The success of the mission relied on him and his partner William Clark getting it right. Their men were convinced it was the North Fork, but having climbed to the overlook, Lewis concluded that its waters weren't clear enough to be fed by the snow-capped peaks that he could see in the distance. Scouting trips up the two forks were inconclusive. Ultimately, the men respected their leaders' position and willingly took the South Fork. They plunged forward for days, despite being utterly unconvinced, before finally hitting the waterfall that confirmed that it was, in fact, the Missouri.

What special blend of acumen, instinct, and raw courage leads to a successful, executable strategy that anticipates and leverages change? Perhaps the answer lies in your ability to find that elevated vantage point, garner the respect to lead people when necessary toward a destination that only you can see, and finally, in Abraham Lincoln's words, to constantly "think anew and act anew" as change inevitably ripples through the plan. ✳

Plan a little; think a lot; decide always.

THINGS TO LISTEN FOR

WHEN STRATEGY IS IN PLACE . . .

"I can see ahead clearly and anticipate how this will play out."

"Building this capability will position us for long-term results."

"When I'm thoughtful I don't have to expend all of my energy, I just have to focus my energy on the right things."

WHEN THERE IS A NEED FOR STRATEGY . . .

"Strategic plans never get executed the way they were intended, so why bother?"

"I can't even get through today's challenges, let alone think ahead and prepare for future challenges."

"There is too much uncertainty. How can I be expected to predict the future?"

IDEAS FOR ACTION

Do

Broadening your Perspective

LEARN ALL ASPECTS OF YOUR BUSINESS It's possible that your own expertise and background are focused in a couple of key business functions. What about the areas of the business where you did not complete a "tour of duty"? Find ways to get a deep understanding of all functions and departments of your business, and how decisions made in one affect the other areas. Thinking of your business as a closed, interdependent system will help you project out the consequences of different approaches.

LEARN FROM THE PAST Past is prologue; study and draw insight from history. Take Ford's strategy with the Model T—how did small incremental improvements in the early models keep costs low? What changed? Seek out books, films, and other literature that study past successes and failures, businesses that thought they had solid strategies right up until the moment they fell off a cliff. Become an astute study of strategic change management.

TAKE TANGENTS Breakthrough ideas and innovation are often the results of tangents, grand detours from your normal flow of information and routines. Find new sources of inspiration. Ask people outside of your line of work for their opinions. Sometimes a non-expert brings fresh perspective and asks straightforward questions that rightfully upend your thinking. Steve Jobs frequently asked one of his friends from Silicon Valley for his opinion on different iterations of *Toy Story* when it was in production. The man was a technology executive, not a filmmaker, but his fresh perspective helped Jobs crystallize his thoughts on how to better develop the film's characters. Finally, some of your best ideas can emerge in the down beats. Einstein, for example, had many breakthroughs while playing Bach on his violin. Often the best solutions form when our minds are relaxed, rested, or focused on activities we enjoy.

Seek out books, films, and other literature that study past successes and failures.

Predicting the Future

PLAY OUT FUTURE SCENARIOS   Imagine the chain reaction of events if you were to set one thing in motion. *If A, then B, then C.* Then add in the contextual variables that you have no control over. If the business goes in this direction and the market behaves this way versus that way, then what can you expect? All of the possible permutations could make your head spin, but at some level, building a strategy that you can stand behind requires you to run through your playbook. And, like a playbook, be pictorial: Visualize through diagrams and charts—name the plays—draw the "*Why*," "*When*," "*Who*," and the paths to the "*What.*"

Once you see it laid out, you can make an informed call. You can't predict the future, but you can perhaps invent it thanks to thoughtful, assured decision-making and clean follow-through.

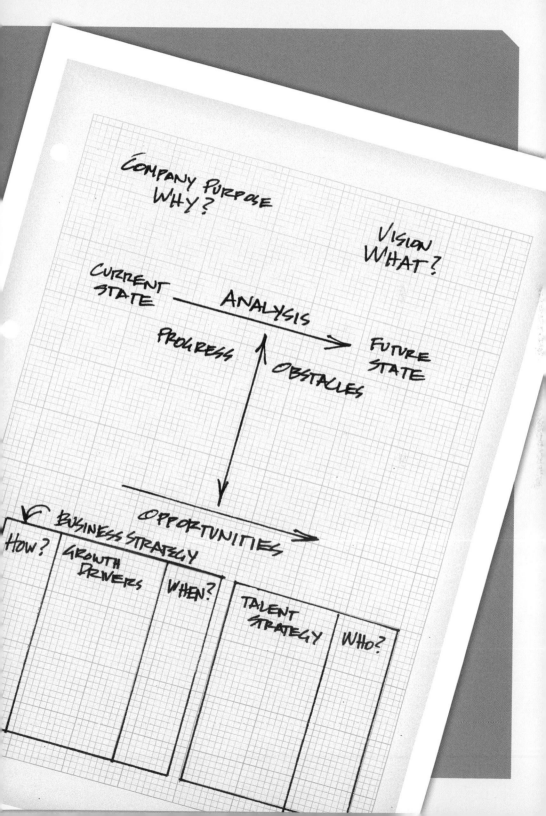

ACCEPT STRATEGY AS DYNAMIC AND PERPETUAL
Some people avoid strategic planning because they think it's
futile given the unruly and unknown chaos of the future, or
they incorrectly believe it's a once-a-year exercise. That's like
throwing your paddles into the water and drifting into class-4
rapids backwards. Strategy demands constant reassessment, and
every master embraces that. Situations change, new information
comes to light, feedback comes in; you evaluate and then iterate.

PREPARE FOR THE WORST-CASE SCENARIO   You may
have seen the popular series of *Worst-Case Scenario Handbooks*,
in which survival strategies are taken to their amusing extreme.
In all seriousness, you need one for your business. Strategic
planning needs to include alternatives for when things don't go
as planned. And, really, who expects 100 percent smooth sailing
these days? Have a Plan C for Plan B.

Acting Strategic to Become More Strategic

MASTER THE LEXICON   Remember one of George Orwell's
most famous insights, that language facilitates thought: "How
could you have a slogan like 'freedom is slavery' when the concept
of freedom has been abolished?" Academics and practitioner-
gurus are constantly creating new ways to think about business
strategy and new words and concepts that describe strategic
thinking—terms like *strategic intent, core capabilities, value
migration, market oligarchy.* Learn the code, learn the concepts,
and your ability to formulate solid strategy will follow.

STUDY STRATEGY Become a student of strategy. As long as you are motivated, you'll find no shortage of material. Read strategic thinkers—Michael Porter, Ram Charan, C.K. Prahalad, to name a few. Attend a strategy course through an executive MBA program. Join the Strategic Leadership Forum. Find a mentor inside or outside your company. Study other companies' strategies by reading annual reports, scanning analyst write-ups and company websites, attending conferences, listening to CEOs, and perusing thought leadership from professional services firms and periodicals such as *Korn/Ferry Briefings* and *Harvard Business Review*. All around you, strategies are formed and unfolding. Let the world become your classroom to observe, ask questions, and draw lessons from other companies strategic successes and failures.

PRACTICE STRATEGY You can practice strategic thinking in real business contexts or in scenario-based contexts. If you're new to strategy, take some time to learn chess, or go to a game store that features brain-building games that build strategic thinking. Find and explore anything that forces you to link several variables together, come up with a likely scenario, and test your projections. Take what you learn from these experiences and apply them. Keep track of your thinking and your results. Don't look to be perfect; instead, seek out ways to continuously evolve. ■

Have a Plan C
for Plan B.

Questions for reflection . . .

Given what I want to achieve, what alternative paths will take us to the destination?

What examples from other industries could help me think this through?

What trends do I see in the world? How will those trends affect my customers?

What problem needs to be solved? What need must be met? What will simplify the lives of customers?

Based on my past experience, what I know to be true, and my gut instinct, what strategy is most likely to succeed in future scenarios?

to choose character over pedigree."

PEOPLE

No matter your industry or functional focus—launching a startup, engineering a turnaround, developing a new market—the people part of your business is where it all starts, piecing all those rough, jagged edges of individuality into one, continuous, unified mosaic of productive excellence. ⇒

"In show business, the show comes first, because if you have a great show, you have a great business. If you don't have a good show, you don't have a business."

Daniel Lamarre, *CEO, Cirque du Soleil*

The mechanics of this essential task garners the most attention: the hiring and the firing, putting the right people with the right skills in the right places at the right time, and helping them work well together. To do this well, start by constantly looking beyond those things trumpeted on their resumes and asking questions that tease out what's *not* on the page: their hunger. Their humanity. Their resilience.

You must remember to choose character over pedigree. In other words, hire for not simply what someone has done but more importantly who they are.

The story of one's character must often be excavated from the white spaces of his or her professional history, in exactly those tales most people leave off their resumes: setbacks, detours, and life-altering

Gauge talent with more sensitive and idiosyncratic indicators than pedigree.

events that involve overcoming adversity. Finding the right players for your team, and quickly letting go those you come to realize are wrong for the job, is the operational dimension to talent management. You can accomplish it by evolving your process and protocols. A dimension of people leadership that's not as easy to address, but perhaps more important, is your own behavior.

Few things are as powerful in determining a company's culture as the daily one-on-one actions of its leadership. In other words, if you want your people to be flexible, adaptable, and open to feedback, so must you be. "Before you can inspire with emotion, you must be swamped with it yourself," said Winston Churchill. "Before you can move their tears, your own must flow. To convince them, you must yourself believe."

Model behavior: Instill a "say/do" ratio of one to one—do what you say, and say what you mean.

The essential ingredient of people leadership is to make an emotional connection on a very real and human level in every interaction. It's not done by force or proclamation but by being the kind of person whose magnetism makes people want to do more and do it better. Of course, we're not all born with a magical and heady mix of charisma, genius, and bravado. But there is one trait you *can* cultivate that I believe is as powerful a magnetic force: *presence*.

In today's world especially, it's a rare thing for a leader, or anybody really, to be thoroughly present in his or her interactions with others. We are in constant movement, yet constantly fear we are behind. Our days feel shorter. Always either in the inbox or the outbox, we walk the streets with our heads down staring into four-inch glowing screens, processing an incessant stream of disembodied communications.

Real attention paid to us in real time—one-to-one, eye-to-eye, genuine, present, and singularly focused on another—has become an experience of such scarcity, that when it's given, it creates the opportunity to influence others intimately, to communicate effectively, and to create in very little time an interpersonal bond that is the basis of teams making things happen they otherwise could not.

Those who have met with former President Bill Clinton remark on his ability to make you feel like *the only person who exists on this fair Earth* while he's speaking with you. Master that feat, and you'll become a celebrated leader yourself.

**Without the talent, there is no show;
let them know it, often.**

Presence is so darn effective because it satisfies the ultimate human desire to be seen, heard, and acknowledged. As Daniel Lamarre, CEO of Cirque du Soleil, which has entertained 100 million people on six continents, once told me, "My ultimate goal is that other people, even if they are all by themselves in an office, will think and act as if there were people watching what they are doing." To be seen is to be motivated. How many times did you say thank you to somebody today? As a leader, you can't say it enough.

Believe it.
Say it.
Mean it.
Act it.

Practice presence to win hearts and minds.

When there is trust in what you say, there will be belief in what you do.

Recognition is an accelerator. If you know that people thrive when someone pays attention, then you must, as a leader, notice and recognize them—consistently and genuinely. Sounds simple; it's not. Try it and after every interaction with an employee, ask yourself a simple question: Does that person feel better after the conversation than before? If not, you have failed.

A good leader is endlessly creative in finding ways to recognize and celebrate the individual and her work. A Steve Jobs story told by Andy Hertzfeld, a member of the development team of the first Apple Macintosh, provides a perfect example. Jobs had the idea of having the signature of everyone on the team engraved on the inside of the original Mac's plastic case. "Most customers would never see them, since you needed a special tool to look inside," writes Hertzfeld, "but we would take pride in knowing that our names were in there, even if no one else knew. We held a special signing party after one of our weekly meetings on February 10, 1982 . . . cake and champagne were served as he called each team member to step forward and sign their name for posterity."

Surely, everyone on the Apple team felt better after that meeting than they did before it. Steve Job's people leadership, on that day, was a success. ✳

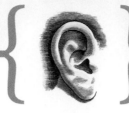

THINGS TO LISTEN FOR

WHEN THERE **IS** A FOCUS ON PEOPLE . . .

"I feel appreciated for what I contribute."

"This company really values its employees."

"If I have an idea that could really improve the business, I know that my leaders are willing to listen."

WHEN THERE **NEEDS** TO BE MORE FOCUS ON PEOPLE . . .

"I don't think the leaders of this company really understand what I do or what my unit does for the business."

"Outside of the annual review process, I don't get much feedback."

"It's hard to get motivated when my efforts go unrecognized."

"Nobody has ever said 'thank you.' They don't even know my name."

IDEAS FOR ACTION

Do

Making the Tough Calls

HAVE AN EYE FOR TALENT "Gut instinct" is grossly over-rated as a selection criterion for good talent. No doubt, there have been times you were sure you made the right call only to be sadly surprised at the outcome. Unfortunately, we all have biases and shortcuts when we're judging other people. Don't let your eyes and your voice judge before your ears listen. To counteract those distortions, be aware of your personal biases. Do you tend to favor people who are similar to you? Are there characteristics that you value too much over others? What downsides do you ignore or explain away? The secret to success lies in specificity. Learn how to describe and appreciate the skills other people, especially those who are not like you, bring to the table.

GIVE FEEDBACK Positive feedback requires you to be generous with your most precious resource: time. Make time to say what you appreciate about people's contributions—and in those moments of recognition, be fully present. It will go a long way to motivating them in the future. Now, making constructive criticism motivational is a much trickier feat. Sandwiching it with a positive message, if delivered with authenticity, can help. (Again, embrace presence.) Be clear about expectations, offer support in meeting those expectations, and restate your belief that the expectations can be met. It's just like that tough grader in college who you worked so hard to impress. Getting a B+ from a tough grader can be more satisfying than an A from an easy grader. People will work hard to make you happy if they know exactly what it takes—and that they'll be recognized when they get there.

KNOW WHEN TO LET THEM GO   It's well-known that "A" players like to work with other "A" players. Think carefully about how your organization treats lower performers. If low performers are coddled, you may not only be stuck with the duds, you may be chasing away the superstars. Make sure you and other leaders are doing everything you can to set people up for success. Set clear goals and objectives, provide coaching and feedback, and offer training and development opportunities when useful. But at the end of the day, if someone is not meeting expectations, you know what you need to do.

Owning Your Talent

KNOW WHO YOU'VE GOT   Of course you know your team, but do you know their teams? What about the rising stars? Know the talent in your organization. You can do this in a formal talent review facilitated by HR, but you can and should do this informally, as well. Ask other leaders who you should get to know, then ask them to lunch or give them a call. Let them know that you want to know the people who work for you—at all levels. Knowing your talent is knowing what your business is capable of. Also, remember that, as in baseball, not every potential high-performer will walk through your door that way; Mike Piazza, the great baseball catcher, was a 62nd-round pick. Provide opportunities to push and develop people along the way.

MATCH PEOPLE TO THE RIGHT ROLE   As a leader, knowing what talent moves make sense for which people is your job. Just as in chess, the best players see many moves ahead; you need to be aware of how the talent moves you facilitate now will help your company's capabilities in the future. The twist is that sometimes the purpose of the match is to shore up critical weaknesses and sometimes the match is to deploy someone's strengths. Consider the needs of the business, the risks the business is willing to take, and whether it's best to place a candidate who can hit the ground running versus someone who needs to be developed for the long run.

BUILD THE BENCH   Having a succession plan for mission-critical roles is something your board puts a high value on. Make sure you are identifying the people with the highest potential for future roles, not just those with good track records. Past performance is only an indicator of future performance when the future looks just like the past—and these days, it rarely does. That being said, don't underestimate the need for bench strength for high professional roles—deep experts provide tremendous competitive advantage for your company.

Motivating Your People

BE RELATABLE   Having an approachable demeanor (presence, presence, presence) is welcoming and reduces the intimidation factor. Relating well to other people by being gracious, pleasant, considerate, and respectful makes people feel valued and important. When people feel valued and important they are more engaged, and they are more likely to open up and share insights and concerns with you. They'll be happier, too, and that's important: Harvard Business School professor Teresa Amabile and developmental psychologist Steven Kramer studied 238 people across seven companies and found that employees generate their most creative ideas when their moods are elevated. Interpersonal skills are often written off as "soft skills," but in actuality they have hard outcomes on your business.

SHARE THE CREDIT Teams win games, coaches lose games. Sharing wins and successes is so critical to building a great team. The reality is that most achievements require a small army of committed and talented collaborators. As a leader, it's your responsibility to personally take accountability for mistakes, and to share the credit for wins—a sort of noblesse oblige. People will respect you for it, and as a result, work harder.

BUILD THE TEAM You may not have the luxury of hand picking your team. But even when you inherit a team, you have the opportunity to identify the unique strengths each team member contributes and to figure out how to get them to work together. Building a team means that the whole is more than the sum of its parts. Make sure that each team member is not just fully utilized, but that his or her strengths are leveraged and colleagues complement him or her. It's also your job to assess what's missing. Is there a skills gap that a new team member could fill? Finding the right balance and blend is dynamic and progressive. ■

Questions for reflection . . .

Who have I neglected to appreciate, out loud?

What efforts have I overlooked?

What can I do to attract and retain the best and the brightest?

How are people at our company deployed? Do their assignments promote their development?

Do I know our talent?

is doing
things right;
leadership
is doing the
right things."

PETER DRUCKER

5

MEASURE
& MO

Peter Drucker's oft-quoted management platitude "what gets measured gets managed" is also oft misunderstood. It's not that it's not true—measurement is essential—but analytics alone can be as damaging as they are productive.

Some things, after all, are pointless to measure—if your goal, say, is to launch a rocket to the moon, you wouldn't measure how many calories the engineering team consumed in a week. ⇒

Measurement allows you to avoid becoming
the leader of the inevitable.

"If you aren't measuring, you're just practicing."

KEVIN PLANK, *CEO, Under Armour*

That's a glib example, but the danger of getting lost in metrics is real, and greater than ever in today's Big Data world, with IT systems enabling every and any organizational minutia to be recorded and spit out in reports that can quickly drown an office in reams of paper. No, instead, the platitude finds its proper context in another of Drucker's sayings: "Management is doing things right; leadership is doing the right things."

To do the right things, you've got to be prepared to tap the radical, intuitive freethinker within yourself—and on your teams— while keeping your inner "nuts and bolts businessperson" perpetually on call. There's no better example of that duality in action than Billy Beane, the general manager of the Oakland A's made famous by the book and movie *Moneyball*, which chronicled his team's 2001–2002 season.

Data is only as useful as your ability to filter and interpret it in context.

Beane, faced with the loss of his three best players after a poor showing in the playoffs the year before, knew he needed to scout and acquire new talent—on a budget that put the big stars well out of reach. Forced to "adapt or die!," as he says in the movie, he stopped thinking about replacing his stars with comparable players, and instead stepped back and asked himself to look more broadly at what it takes to *win games.* With that new focus, he dumped the "five tools" criteria that all scouts use and instead relied on computer-generated statistical analysis. Beane's wildly successful method showed that the old metrics weren't necessarily the right ones.

Note that the subtitle of Michael Lewis' book is *The Art of Winning an Unfair Game*—the *art,* not the science. Data is important, but flexible thinking and intuitive leadership is the art that you must master to make the data useful. Start from the premise that, as management educator Henry Mintzberg has said, "You can't measure what matters." Coming at it from that point of view puts the right weight on your responsibility to go beyond the numbers, asking *what, why,* and *where to from here,* if you want to break records.

The kind of data you need to stay on top of *what matters* doesn't come from numbers but people. It's not the stuff of spreadsheets and charts; it's the information you can only get when you ask people to be candid and listen to what they have to say. It's feedback. It's not always easy to hear, but it's always helpful.

As part of a recent leadership meeting at Korn/Ferry, I called my direct reports together and asked them to spend two hours with me, rating my strengths, blind spots, and weaknesses. They used clickers

Scrutinize losses as much as wins.

Open your ears to what you don't want to hear; create a culture that does the same.

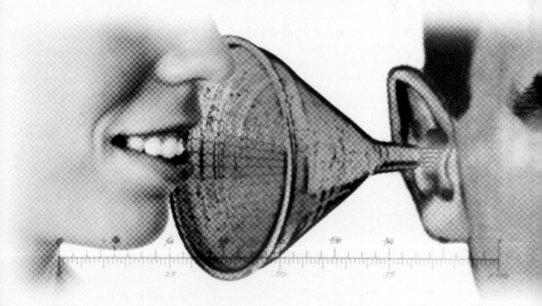

Self-satisfaction corrupts your data and stifles innovation; feedback is the antidote.

for anonymity, but I received the feedback in real time. As the session closed and opened, I told them, "It starts with you and me."

The experience was grueling—and incredible, thanks to the quality of the feedback I received, and even more importantly, the message it sent to the team. They left with the full understanding that leadership at our company—not just mine, but theirs—means having the courage to ask for and listen to criticism and honest feedback.

If you want good data and even better ideas, you need a company culture that gives them to you. Self-satisfied leadership creates a self-satisfied team that chugs along complacently—good enough to do things right, but unlikely to do the right things. So it's up to you to take the risk and ask for feedback, in as public a company forum as you can.

Make it safe, explicitly, for others to illuminate your blind spots—if not with the drama of a group 360, then one on one. If you don't, the blind spots will still be there, and everyone else in your company will be comfortable ignoring them right along with you. All the numbers will add up—to nothing.

Open your ears to what you don't want to hear, create a culture that does the same, and you'll have exactly the "data" you need to complement the numbers that matter. ✳

**Performance is not absolute; it's relative.
It starts with you—and ends with them.**

THINGS TO LISTEN FOR

WHEN THERE **IS** A FOCUS ON MEASURE & MONITOR . . .	WHEN THERE **NEEDS** TO BE MORE FOCUS ON MEASURE & MONITOR . . .
"I know exactly what my progress is toward my goals."	"These reports have so many data points it's difficult to make sense of them, let alone act on them."
"Hearing from stakeholders and customers helps me make adjustments to what we're doing."	"I like what we've been able to accomplish, but I couldn't tell you exactly what our customers think."
"Measuring progress helps our teams know which initiatives are working."	"I'm not sure how I will know if I'm getting closer to our goal."

IDEAS FOR ACTION

Do

Setting Goals

DEFINE WHAT SUCCESS LOOKS LIKE Goal setting is not rocket science, but for some reason people find it difficult to do. You've probably heard of SMART goals—goals that are specific, measurable, actionable, realistic, and time-bound. Often, the issue is that one or more of these areas is difficult to pin down—is there anyone who can help you with that? Specificity is mandatory; it's impossible to measure progress if you don't know the target. Saying that you want your business to be global is vague and not measurable. Stating that you want 25 percent of your revenue to come from outside North America by the end of the next fiscal year is better. It's a clear stake in the ground. And, it motivates people to figure out how to make it happen.

> Specificity is mandatory; it's impossible to measure progress if you don't know the target.

ENGAGE THE TEAM Dictating goals to people in your organization is not especially motivating. At the same time, you can't have every department or team deciding on the direction of the organization. Think about how to engage others in the goal-setting process. Ask people what they think is possible and realistic. Gather all that good, nuanced data and use it to help you craft goals that can be cascaded throughout the organization, aligning efforts across departments and business units.

MATCH THE GOALS TO THE PERSON People are different and teams are different. Take these facts into consideration as you set goals for them. Consider a 2008 study at Chicago University's Graduate School of Business: Researchers found that teams with a weak level of motivation to achieve a given goal performed better when told how much progress they had already made. Highly motivated teams, meanwhile, got a bigger boost from focusing on how much work still needed to be done. Similarly, consider the team's collective mindset when considering how much "stretch" should be in the goals you set. Will they be energized or demotivated? Make sure that the goal and the way it's communicated are motivating. Meet people where they are, not where you want to be.

Choosing the Right Metrics

MEASURE WHAT MATTERS Once your goals are set, make sure that what you are monitoring is relevant and contributes directly to achieving them. Also remember that what matters can be extremely unique to your company; don't be afraid to "Billy Beane" what everyone else is doing. The shoe company Zappos, to give an example, has thrown most traditional performance metrics out the door and focuses on the science of happiness to create employee and customer delight—an approach that few would have predicted would result in more than $1 billion in gross sales, profitability, and world renown for CEO Tony Hsieh.

ESTABLISH A DASHBOARD Often it takes more than one metric to gauge progress. In fact, in isolation some metrics can be counterintuitive. For example, one key business metric for retailers is conversion—out of 100 customers walking through the doors, how many buy something? One store could have sky-high conversion rates, but does that help you understand if you are making a profit on that store? Not necessarily. Conversion needs to be added to a number of other measures including average transaction, gross margin, and labor costs (among other things) to gauge whether the store is achieving its goal of being profitable. Pulling a set of metrics into a dashboard can provide an at-a-glance set of data that fills in a more complete picture of progress.

USE METRICS TO MOTIVATE ACTION Researchers Teresa Amabile and Steven Kramer, whom I referenced in an earlier chapter, have identified progress as one of the most important yet

"Test fast; fail fast; adjust fast."

Tom Peters

underemphasized motivators for employees. Give as much feedback on progress as possible. Make it visual. Create infographics and color-coded charts. Once people gauge their pace and progress, they know where to step up the effort in order to move the needle—but they want and need to see it move. Help people visualize progress, so that they can, as Tom Peters says, "Test fast, fail fast, adjust fast."

Gathering Rich Feedback

DISCOVER WHAT IS BEHIND THE NUMBERS Sometimes numbers are the tip of the iceberg, and sometimes numbers mask what's actually happening behind the scenes. If you want to have a clear sense of what the numbers mean, get the back story. Gather qualitative data—anecdotes that bring texture and meaning to the metrics. If you see sales are up in a certain region, ask why. Maybe there is some temporary need that is driving it, or

The accountability you want to see in others starts with you.

maybe it's a new permanent customer need that is being fulfilled. Knowing the back story will help you make business decisions so that you don't overinvest or leave money on the table.

Make sure, as well, to stay connected to the ground. Imagine yourself as the manager of a factory: While poring over report data with your office door closed tight, you might not hear the shift from a hum to a groan that immediately speaks to a failure in the machinery. So keep that door open and listen for the hum—or tap its human equivalent. Ford CEO Alan Mulally once told the *Wall Street Journal* that his strategic process involves talking to hundreds of individuals from the employee, industry, and dealer ranks to inform his strategy. "When you get that much input from that many stakeholders, you get really good, robust feedback about the way it is," he said. "So you take that and develop a strategy and a plan to deal with that reality."

ASK FOR FEEDBACK Once again, self-scrutiny from the top down creates the kind of company that recognizes and reports those "failures in the machinery," and that meets change with creativity and confidence. Look in the mirror every day, and ask people to be honest with you. Ask them frequently, kindly, and in as many ways as possible. Recognize that it takes a lot of courage for people to give feedback to a leader. They may weigh the risks and benefits and decide they'd rather stay quiet. You must create a climate where people can be open with you about personal feedback as well as feedback about how the business is operating. Be calm and nonreactive, show that candid feedback is rewarded, and give employees ample time and opportunity to practice candor.

LISTEN FOR STORIES Stories can be as telling as data. You've heard the distinction between the letter of the law and the spirit of the law. Here we have the letter of the goal versus the spirit of the goal. You may be making your numbers on the dashboard, but stories will reveal the costs and benefits behind that progress, and whether the organization's values are being upheld even while the business goals are being met. ■

Questions for reflection . . .

What should I or the organization do more or less of?

How will I know if we're on track?

What milestones do we want to reach, by when?

What story do the data tell?

What's behind the data?

Why are the data trending the way they are?

"DELEGATE almost

to the point of
abdication."

WARREN BUFFETT

INSPIRE &

EMPOWER

Peter Guber, Hollywood mogul and producer of films such as *Rain Man* and *Midnight Express*, tells this story: Back in the 1980s, he was looking for a studio to finance a project that screamed "Pass!" to everyone who read it: female lead, expensive African location, gorillas, and a very unhappy ending. The script was *Gorillas in the Mist*, and as we all know today, it was ultimately produced to great critical acclaim and four Oscar nods. But at the time, the script was a hot potato. ⇒

"Who's going to want to see a movie about a gorilla?" Warner Brothers CEO Terry Semel initially told Guber.

But Guber told Semel he had it all wrong. *Gorillas* was really about "shining a light on the fact that these creatures are only one click away in the gene pool from us. We're their partner on this planet." Furthermore, Guber believed in the project so much that he'd put his own money into it.

With that new twist on the story, Semel bit.

Guber, author of *Tell to Win: Connect, Persuade, and Triumph with the Hidden Power of Story*, relates the tale frequently while illustrating what it takes to motivate someone to action. As he once told me, "Leadership is storytelling in a way that becomes memorable and actionable. Storytelling is as old as human beings. About 40,000 years ago, if we [hadn't] worked together and used language, we wouldn't have survived. So you could say leadership is a 40,000-year-old process."

You don't have to be Dorothy Parker or Bill Clinton or, for that matter, Peter Guber. The most essential ingredient to telling stories that are, as Guber puts it, "emotional transportation," is your own authenticity. You need stories that you can own. Authenticity trumps charisma any day. As the leader, you don't just deliver the message—

Stories are emotional transportation, and authenticity trumps charisma.

you *are* the message. "If you want to move somebody, you've got to have your feet, your heart, your wallet, and your tongue going in the same direction," says Guber. "As soon as they see those things going in different directions, you don't seem authentic."

People must be able to feel your sincerity—and see that transformed into actions. Whatever lofty notions are shuttling around your head about the kind of leader you want to be, remember Aristotle: "We become just by performing just actions, temperate by performing temperate actions, brave by performing brave actions." When people feel the force of your passion and commitment, in the stories you tell and the actions those stories reflect, they open themselves to connecting deeply. People will believe—and be inspired to action.

Beyond authenticity, look to infuse your stories with emotion and the full, rich detail of your experience. Scientists who study the brain's response to narrative have found that a story told with descriptive language isn't merely processed in the language center of the organ, but in the parts of the brain that process real-life smells, sounds, and other stimuli. In other words, a story can create a true emotional sense memory, and those are the ones that stick around to influence future actions. That level of story can only come from you—your tone, body language, and your choice of words. Forget Twitter for now.

Emotionalize your message to move others to consider what they, too, might become if they were "more"—more determined, more prepared, more confident, and more empowered. An easy way to do that is to write them into the story, with all the research that requires:

Empowering your team requires you to relinquish some control.

Who are they, what do they care about, and where does it fit into the grand epic of your work together? To inspire, you've got to make sure that even those who apparently have bit parts understand that at some key moment, it is nevertheless their work that drives the plot.

Here's why this is all so important: Empowerment isn't something you can gift like an engraved paperweight. People empower themselves and so as the leader, your job is to motivate them to feel, think, and act—and then to step far enough away from the action to allow them to own the process. Flex your Warren Buffett muscle and "delegate almost to the point of abdication." Charge them with results rather than with specific tasks in order to create the excitement of a challenge that can be met *if and only if* they bring their unique creativity to bear.

Above all, remember, it's not power, it's *em*power. Learn restraint and worry less about protecting your authority. If your team is so inspired and excited that they demand to do things their way, you've won the most important battle and can enjoy the skirmish.

A team's engagement is directly proportionate to the leader's ability to inspire. Help them along even further by being behind them in success and in front of them in defeat. Establish a culture that learns lessons from failure—that's the only way to tap real potential, which by definition means they haven't yet arrived at their biggest win. Enable and equip, and then get out of their way. You can't just say, "People are our most valuable resource." Show it. Make *their* success *your* priority. ☀

**Inspire your team to action,
then get out of the way.**

THINGS TO LISTEN FOR

WHEN THERE **IS** A FOCUS ON EMPOWER & INSPIRE . . .	WHEN THERE **NEEDS** TO BE MORE FOCUS ON EMPOWER & INSPIRE . . .
"I believe in what we're doing here and I know that my work makes a difference."	"Even if I did work harder, what would it accomplish?"
"It's up to each one of us to make the vision a reality."	"Where I work isn't important—it's a paycheck."
"I feel motivated to go above and beyond."	"I'm not sure if I'll still be at this company in a couple years."

Make both failures and victories empowering milestones to success.

IDEAS FOR ACTION

Do

Keeping It Real

BE HONEST AND AUTHENTIC To inspire others, your vision of the future needs to be backed by your own energy and commitment. If you're not motivated from within, you need to dig deeper or find a new role. This doesn't mean silencing your doubts, hesitations, or wishful thinking; it means peppering them into the narrative. That level of honesty is essential, even seductive. Enthusiasm without honesty is anathema to success.

TAP INTO WHAT MOTIVATES YOU AND OTHERS   Respect that motivation is highly individual. What gets one person out of bed has another hitting "snooze" or even "self-destruct." In order to inspire people to rally around a common vision, you need to find and tap into all of the different reasons people would be motivated to work toward that vision. Ask yourself, ask other people—what motivates you? As you interact with people, watch what makes their eyes light up, and get them talking about it until you find a way to genuinely connect it back to your work together.

PAINT A PICTURE   Think of the speeches you sat through that left you feeling energized and ready for action—or even just the few that you still remembered 24 hours later. It's almost a given that the person offered clear examples, used metaphors to bring ideas to life, and told stories rich with detail and flourishes. As Tom Peters has written, "Very near the heart of the Technicolor spirit is . . . Technicolor Language." If you don't trust your storytelling ability, or if you can't think of relevant stories to drive your point home, use a crutch—find an impactful video to get your point across or ask someone else to tell their story as part of your presentation. Do whatever it takes to create an experience that emotionally, compellingly drives home the vision you are trying to bring to life.

Delegating

YOU DECIDE "WHAT." THEY DECIDE "HOW." Being told what to do and how to do it is incredibly disempowering. But that doesn't mean leaving the orchestra flying into cacophony without a conductor. Your role is to *set expectations around results,* with as much specificity as you can offer. Then, let each person choose a plan of action, based on his or her unique strengths and style. Resist the urge to jump in immediately if you see the person struggling. That level of ownership builds confidence, pride, and accountability, and ultimately helps people feel like they are collaborators in the greater vision. Embrace this opportunity to share the burden, and the joy, of leadership.

DON'T MICROMANAGE Once you've delegated something, step away. You're turning wine back into water if you swoop in and question or criticize a person's approach. He or she may not be ready for your input, and his or her thoughts may not yet be fully formed. To delegate well means giving the person space. Assess the person's ability and willingness to take on the work, and set deliberate milestones for direction or coaching, rather than managing reactively.

DELEGATE TO DEVELOP PEOPLE Ideally, you'll delegate strategically, rather than because you've suddenly discovered that your hydra is short a head. Take stock of your talent and what motivates them, have development conversations, and understand what experiences they long for. After considering what needs to be achieved, carefully match projects to people. In some cases, timelines or other constraints may require you to find a person who's been there, done that, and written the ebook. But if you're good, and developing your talent with an eye on the horizon, you'll create space and take calculated risks to allow for assignments that provide a certain amount of stretch.

Maximizing the Learning Curve

BUILD A RISK-TOLERANT BUSINESS PLAN You've been taught to minimize risk and failure, and that's good sense. But the reality is that failures are going to happen, and the only way to risk nothing is to do nothing. Some ventures rocket; others sputter and die. When building a business plan, a project plan, or any kind of roadmap, factor in a certain amount of failure. Build enough cushion that you can afford the patience to look at failures as investments in learning. Do that and your people will perform at their highest level—fear-free, innovative, and empowered.

Self-awareness and honesty go hand in hand.

MAKE SENSE OF MISTAKES AND FAILURES Once you create a "budget" for mistakes and failures, get your money's worth. People's urge to distance themselves from blame can squelch the learning opportunity it creates. Do whatever you can to take that out of the equation so that a careful, honest analysis can lead to better, more preventative solutions. That's the key to a team that improves and iterates, and never, ever makes the same mistake twice.

LET GO Watching someone make those initially shaky steps toward mastering new skills takes discipline and patience. According to Korn/Ferry's research, patience ranks 62nd out of 67 leadership skills. I think it is one of the world's most valuable, rarely seen, and least celebrated leadership traits. It's a challenge to practice patience when we are watching people struggle, particularly when we shoulder the responsibility for success. But it is in struggle that true learning occurs. Let go of your need to control the outcome or "save" someone else. In moments when you would normally complete someone's thought or jump in to provide the answer to a problem, stop and take a breath. Wait and see if they arrive at a solution. Frustration and struggle are stages of the learning curve, and you'll be ahead in the big picture if you step back enough to develop your team's talent. ∎

Questions for reflection . . .

How can I tell a story that will capture what I want to convey?

Am I adjusting my tone and message for the audience?

Do I believe in what I'm saying?

Am I fired up about our company's future?

What motivates me most?

What motivates other individuals most?

7

is not who you are.”

REWARD & CELE

The number one reason for divorce in America: money. The source of countless wars throughout history: money. What does it take to be President of the United States: money, and a lot of it—how about needing to raise $1 billion for a job that pays $400,000 a year, puts you in the world's tiniest bubble, turns your hair gray (except for Ronald Reagan thanks to tubes of Grecian Formula) and makes half the world disagree with you—no matter what you do. ⇒

BRATE

Money is like water. It is necessary and in many parts of the world it is in short supply; it has a purpose, but it's not durable; and in excess, it's overly visible and utterly destructive.

I recently asked a former member of the President's Cabinet "What was the most surprising thing about Washington, D.C.?" He didn't blink an eye and immediately responded, "The singular goal of the people on the outside is to be back on the inside, and the only objective of the people on the inside is not to be back on the outside." A sad commentary but probably truer than we would like to believe. Power is all too often seated to the right hand of money.

But I have a different view: Money can rent loyalty, but it can't buy it. If money is the only thing that is keeping employees at your company, you'll only keep them until someone else makes a higher offer.

And yet, many managers hear "reward" and automatically jump to money. In fact, money is only the most expensive and least motivating currency circulating in the twenty-first century workplace. Even worse, typical money-based reward systems have been shown to produce a multitude of negative outcomes: poorer performance, diminished creativity, and reduced interest in tasks that were once intrinsically interesting, to name just a few detailed in Dan Pink's excellent *Drive*, a well-researched, forward-thinking examination of employee psychology that shows that "carrot and stick" reward systems are anathema to the real subtlety of how and why rewards affect knowledge workers.

You must win hearts and minds, not buy pocketbooks.

To give one rather counterintuitive example, you might guess that the bigger the performance bonus, the greater the effect. Not so. In a study at CalTech, scientists found that above a certain size, the potential for a bonus *negatively* affected participants' ability to succeed at a simple arcade game. The phenomena seems to be explained by so-called "loss aversion"—the well-documented human propensity to hurt more when we lose than to feel good when we win. The more reward on the line, the more the participants focused on losing—and lose they did.

In another study, at the London School of Economics, financial incentives for performance were found to have a negative effect on overall performance because they can "reduce intrinsic motivation and diminish ethical or other reasons for complying with workplace social norms such as fairness."

The best rewards enhance autonomy, mastery, and purpose.

"[If] the employee doesn't trust you . . . engagement is one-tenth of what it could potentially be. You have to create a culture of trust, and that can happen only by pushing the envelope of transparency."

VINCENT NAYAR, *Vice Chairman, HCL Technologies Ltd.*

In my sixth year as a CEO, I'm not naïve—how people are paid certainly influences how they behave. More important, however, is to ensure that pay is equitable within an organization. Business management psychologist Frederick Herzberg first articulated the idea that "hygiene factors"—such as salary, security, and status— were crucial for avoiding job dissatisfaction, but had little impact on job satisfaction. In other words, you want to pay employees enough so that money is their least concern at the workplace—but to motivate, reward, and celebrate them, the buck (literally) stops elsewhere.

In the knowledge economy we depend on employees to bring their best ideas, creativity, and collaborative impulses into their work. This is not the assembly line, and the way we reward and celebrate workers changes accordingly. So what are today's workers after?

If people join your organization for money alone, they will leave it for money.

Look to maximize three things, according to Pink:

- AUTONOMY: "the desire to direct our own lives;"
- MASTERY: "the urge to make progress and get better at something that matters;" and
- PURPOSE: "the yearning to do what we do in the service of something larger than ourselves."

Compensation packages, while important, are actually secondary to the employees' desire to be challenged, to contribute, to be recognized, and to understand how their actions are contributing to progress for the organization. People want to know that they belong, that they are an integral part of something that is bigger than themselves.

Consider a fundraising call center referenced in *Drive*. When a group of employees was reminded of the personal benefit of working in a call center, they matched the control group in money raised. A second group was asked to read about what their work accomplished—and these people received twice as many pledges. "A brief reminder of the purpose of their work," writes Pink, "doubled their performance."

To autonomy, mastery, and purpose, I'd add a related fourth. For a moment, throw out the footnoted, peer-reviewed studies and simplify the world's motivations to two: "for love or for money." In this dichotomy, love wins out every time.

Celebrations are most valuable when they uniquely and creatively express your appreciation.

You might think that bringing the idea of "love" into your management strategy won't work unless you're in the organic ice cream business, or something similarly soft and squishy. "I double-dog dare you," management expert Gary Hamel told BigThink.com, "go into your next company meeting and say, 'What we really need in this organization is, we need more love.'"

The recoil from "love" in a workplace context is understandable—and yet the most potent rewards, the most meaningful celebrations, share this root characteristic. They make the employee feel loved. Love, here, is being held by a community that appreciates and celebrates each other deeply and personally; by a community that trusts each other to do the right thing; by a community that supports its members' autonomy, mastery, and purpose.

Leaders need followers, and emotion remains the most powerful means to change minds, by gaining access through the heart and then following it with reason. Why should relationships in business be any different from any other relationship? When the leader communicates, "We couldn't have done it without you" what he is really saying to each contributor is, "You are loved."

Letting employees know that you genuinely, personally appreciate them means going beyond whatever might be promised in their contracts. Informal recognition should be constant and tailored to the employee and the situation at hand—a handwritten note, a simple "thank you." You can never say "I believe in you" too often. Celebrate the incremental achievements, not only the final results. The most memorable part of the destination is always the journey—that's what people remember most, the quality and rigor of experiences along the way. ✳

THINGS TO LISTEN FOR

WHEN THERE **IS** A FOCUS ON REWARD & CELEBRATE . . .	WHEN THERE **NEEDS** TO BE MORE FOCUS ON REWARD & CELEBRATE . . .
"Nice work."	"I don't know if my efforts make a difference."
"I really felt appreciated."	
"We couldn't have done it without you."	"Celebrating team effort always gets so political around here."
"I believe in you."	"I can't remember the last time my boss paused and said, 'Nice work.'"

Do

IDEAS FOR ACTION

Balancing Reward and Consequence

FOLLOW THROUGH You stated your expectations. You stated what it would look like if expectations were missed, met, or exceeded. You probably also gave some indication of what was at stake and what the consequences were. Now follow through. Measure what you said you would measure. Hold people accountable. Holding people accountable takes discipline, but *your* reward is that when they meet and exceed your expectations, you get to deliver positive feedback. Celebrate those who exceeded the goal, compliment the ones who just eked it out, and have a serious, sit-down discussion with those who missed the target. Following through means you being taken seriously next time you state expectations.

BE A TOUGH GRADER It may seem counterintuitive, but it motivates people when they know you have high standards. If you were to compliment every small effort, gradually the time, energy, and thought people put into their work will flatten out. As a tough grader, when you give praise for outstanding work, people will know that you mean it and adjust their efforts accordingly.

REMEMBER THE SANDWICH PRINCIPLE Sandwich difficult feedback and consequences with some hopeful message. Think of a positive, deliver the negative, and follow up with another hopeful positive—and make sure that both praise and critique are sincerely delivered. "I have seen you make a lot of progress. These results were not on target—I expect more than this. But, I know you have ideas on what to do differently next time." People need to hear many more times the number of positive messages to balance out the negative. Don't worry about the constructive feedback getting lost—it makes a lasting impression. So much so that it's important to temper it.

Celebrating Successes

CELEBRATE EVEN SMALLS WINS As Teresa Amabile, co-author of *The Progress Principle: Using Small Wins to Ignite Joy, Engagement, and Creativity at Work,* told Dan Pink, "Our research showed that, of all the events that have the power to excite people and engage them in their work, the single most important is making progress—even if that progress is a small win. That's the progress principle. And, because people are more creatively productive when they are excited and engaged, small wins are a very big deal for organizations." And yet, when Amabile and her co-author asked nearly 700 managers around the world to rank what they thought most motivated employees from five factors, they put progress dead last!

BRING IN THE EXPERTS You hire consultants to help you with business strategy. It might not be a bad idea to bring in recognition experts. There are consulting firms that specialize in recognition. Bringing in the experts can help you do a quick audit of what's working and what's not in your organization. They can offer a fresh infusion of ideas to kick-start a recognition program that's right for your company's culture.

ENCOURAGE GRASSROOTS EFFORTS Often, the best ideas for recognition and celebrating success come from the team members themselves (remember, *autonomy*). Consider setting aside a small budget for ideas that come up after a project team meets a major milestone. Whether it's dinner out, a golf tournament, or some other outing, it's likely that the cost of celebrating is paid back with dividends when it comes to engaged team members who are ready to tackle the next challenge.

BUILD A CULTURE OF RECOGNITION Once you find what's meaningful for your employees and right for your company, find ways to ingrain it into your company culture—even physically. What do visitors see when they walk through the building? Is there any evidence that you are a company that celebrates success and recognizes the people who make it possible?

Remember Rewards and Recognition Do's and Don'ts

IT'S NOT ONE-SIZE-FITS ALL Don't assume that you know what motivates people. Ask them. Values are different. Some people value work environment and the content of their work over everything else. Figuring out ways to remove roadblocks and obstacles will engage these folks. Others may like different types of perks—a reserved parking spot, flexible work hours, floating holidays, support for working remotely . . . the list goes on and on. Empower managers to have conversations with their direct reports about what matters most, and if it's within reason, find ways to reward high performing employees in a way that means something to them.

DO AWAY WITH "IF-THEN" REWARDS Contingent rewards ("if you do this, then you get that") are the ones that negatively affect performance—because, according to Pink, they undermine autonomy. Therefore, extrinsic rewards should be announced only *after* a task is done, and not so often that such a bonus becomes expected.

IT'S NOT ABOUT THE MONEY When it comes to engagement, compensation matters but it's never at the top of the list. In fact, trust in senior leaders and a positive relationship with one's immediate boss are the factors most linked to engagement scores. Certainly, pay fairness is a factor and your company will need to meet the threshold for people to be committed to staying. But job satisfaction and engagement depend on many other variables that your company can control. Remember Pink: How can you enhance their autonomy, mastery, and sense of purpose?

DON'T IGNORE THE FUN FACTOR Especially in tough times, it's hard to keep a sense of humor and remember to have fun. It's up to you to help your team find the balance. When people have fun at work and enjoy the people they work with, their engagement, and with it, performance, skyrockets. When it comes to rewarding and celebrating, think one part Winston Churchill, one part Alfred Nobel, two parts Groucho Marx. Take it seriously, but don't be so serious. ■

Questions for reflection . . .

How can I let people know that I appreciate their work?

Am I spending more time sharing criticism or praise?

Do I know how my team members like to be rewarded for their contribution?

Have I avoided celebrating team efforts because I'm worried about fairness?

How can I foster a culture that appreciates and celebrates contribution?

"LEADERSHIP

is knowing what to do, when you don't know what to do."

ANTI

CIPATE

Thanks to the ever-increasing velocity of change in today's endlessly interconnected world, the immediate future holds both more threats and more opportunities than at any time in history. And that's why *anticipation*, the ability to see the road ahead and act intelligently on the insights that vision reveals, has become so critical. ⇒

The surprising fact is that many leaders are actually not that good at anticipating. The reason it seems to be such a rare skill is that even paragons of strategy fall victim to tunnel vision. IBM failed to recognize the massive market for operating systems that would be created by the emergence of the PC. (The beneficiary of IBM's oversight was Microsoft.) Sony couldn't imagine that VHS might pose some competition to its superior video recording product, Betamax. GM failed to anticipate how unstable oil prices would drive a new market for smaller cars.

Overly focused on short-term financial projections, operational excellence, and the legacy of what they've done before, even the best companies can lose their power of anticipation. In other words, these companies became too focused on the *probable* changes in the

Foster a culture of world-class observers.

outside environment, and lost their awareness of *possible* changes. That's the essence of anticipation: being prepared not just for what might happen, but what you'd *never* expect to happen.

To get anticipation right, you need to develop and practice Wayne Gretsky-style awareness of everything happening outside of and around your business. Gretsky frequently invoked his father's advice, *skate to where the puck is headed, not to where it's been.* But that's only the most superficial explanation of Gretsky's legendary skill, which allowed him to thrive as the world's scrawniest, least technically gifted hockey player.

The more subtle part is the *how*—how did he always know where the puck was headed? The answer, explained in Vivek Ranadivé and Kevin Maney's *The Two-Second Advantage: How We Succeed by Anticipating the Future—Just Enough,* was that Gretsky developed an almost omniscient view of the game in real-time as he was playing it. "I couldn't beat people with my strength; I don't have a hard shot; I'm not the quickest skater in the league," said Gretsky, quoted in the book. "My eyes and my mind have to do most of the work."

Gretzky built a predictive model of hockey in his head, combining past experience and a reading of the immediate situation, he knew where every player was, where they were headed. He had just a little bit more information just a little bit ahead of everyone else, and that made all the difference in the world.

This ability isn't an inevitable quality of genius. After all, plenty of brilliant leaders have failed at it. When IBM lost the desktop com-

You don't need to be the smartest person in the room, just the most aware.

puting market to Microsoft, one might have assumed that Microsoft was uniquely adept at anticipation. But not long after, Microsoft failed to "get" the Internet, and lost the chance at a competitive edge in browsers, search, and any number of other markets that proved to be essential to the online age. Anticipation is as much a cultivated habit, or acquired skill, of peripheral awareness, as it is an innate ability. No matter how well you do what you did, you can never rest on that—someone needs to be responsible for being forever humble, canny, and curious. And as usual as a leader, that "someone" is you.

Going back to Gretsky, it could be argued that he had a major advantage, in that the hockey rink looks to be a closed circuit. But that's not really the case—new players constantly enter the game, teams develop new skills and new strategies. But because Gretsky's knowledge of the game and the action on the rink was so thorough, he could identify and adapt to anything.

Because anticipation plays in the world of possibility, it should be informed by but can't quite be mastered with a quantitative approach. Which is where intuition comes into play. Intuition is too often dismissed as something soft and intangible. Instead, think of it as your body's physical memory, or a kind of imprint, of everything you've learned from every experience you've ever had.

Your body, not your mind, turns out to be the best synthesizer of that volume and delicacy of experience. Intuition—created by mental maps and thousands of hours of game-time decision-making—told Gretsky where the puck was going. Intuition, earned in 30-plus years

Change the mindset from "this is what we have always done" to "this is what we could do now."

of piloting, told Chesley Burnett "Sully" Sullenberger III how to deal with a situation he'd never encountered and land his Airbus A320-214 in the Hudson River to save the lives of 155 passengers when geese blew out the engines.

Know your company and your business to the point where your intuition is honed—then keep your eyes darting to the periphery. The first piece takes depth of knowledge, which you can supplement by pulling quality information from others. As the leader, establish routines and processes that will anchor the organization in real-time data and facts. Also create a culture of candor that welcomes the truth and makes anticipation a team sport, so that ideas bubble up instead of cascading down. Ineffective leadership is not knowing anything about everything; effective leadership is acknowledging what you don't know.

Always have a Plan B—and a backup for the backup.

"We need to sustain growth, not just sustain what has come before so that we're living in the past."

WARREN BENNIS
Distinguished Professor of Business Administration,
University of Southern California

The other half of the job, developing that canny peripheral vision, is largely a matter of cultivating the habit, which you can do fairly quickly. You need not be omnipresent, but you need to be well informed and savvy, scanning up and down and around between the horizon and today, and always focusing on the important rather than the urgent. As a leader, you must encourage creativity by allowing new ideas to be explored, even if they never take flight. There is no failure, after all, except failing to fail.

Above all, beware the seven worst words in corporate speak: "That's the way we've always done it." Embrace a new mantra: "What does tomorrow hold?" ✳

Don't ignore intuition;
you know more than you think you do.

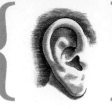

THINGS TO LISTEN FOR

WHEN THERE **IS** A FOCUS ON ANTICIPATE . . .	WHEN THERE **NEEDS** TO BE MORE FOCUS ON ANTICIPATE . . .
"I know this seems unrelated, but let's think for a moment how it might impact our business."	"Our business results surprised us. We didn't realize the shift happening in the marketplace."
"Everyone here is so well-read and aware of current events, it's really helpful in shaping and amending strategy."	"Customer needs changed dramatically—in retrospect, we should have seen it coming."
"Different perspectives are really valued here."	"The global issues we read about in the papers really aren't that relevant for our business."

IDEAS FOR ACTION

Do

Becoming a Master Observer

LEARN FROM HISTORY Studying the past is a great way to see how seemingly unrelated events were actually interconnected, and in some cases created a domino effect that affected businesses. Who would have guessed that during the Gold Rush, the person selling shovels would make more money than most gold panners? Maybe that makes sense now, but it wasn't something people anticipated then. How can you build wisdom from what in retrospect makes sense? How can you project yourself into the future in order to evaluate what you should be anticipating now? How can you sense the hidden opportunity in ongoing trends?

SEE CONNECTIONS Observe what's happening in the world. Read trade publications and periodicals, and not just those targeted to your own industry. Pick a few interesting topics and think about what effect they may have on your organization. Learn to connect what's out there with what's going on in your business.

GET CURIOUS Dabble in things that seem entirely unrelated to your business. Go to the opera, read a novel, learn a new language, travel somewhere you've never been, build something in your garage. By expanding your perspective, you may find a tangent that is actually relevant. Maybe it provides a metaphor that furthers your thinking. Maybe there's a business model that you can apply from a different industry. Maybe there's a linkage that you didn't see before. A curious disposition can help you anticipate because your thinking is less restricted.

Thinking in Possibility

ASK WHY NOT Leaders who are most able to adapt to change and bring their organizations with them tend to ask "why not?" instead of "why?" Using "why not?" as a filter for brainstorming and idea generation can lead you and your team to surprising places. "Why not?" suspends judgment and allows for some more outlandish, impractical ideas to enter into the conversation. Having the freedom to think in possibility—again, this is a much broader realm than *probability*—brings to light ideas and unique connections that may provide expected insight into future trends.

FOLLOW THE IMPROV PRINCIPLE When actors are on stage performing improv, there is an unspoken code of conduct. When one actor builds something from her imagination, the other actors always confirm it and work with it. The creative process builds and does not get stunted by people saying, "I don't see the skyscraper you're looking at" or, "You're not an astronaut, where is your space suit?" Actors instead take the idea and build upon it. Businesses that want to get better at anticipating would be well-served to use the improv principle in brainstorming sessions. Affirming ideas and perspectives and then building upon them can lead to powerful thinking.

QUIET YOUR INNER CRITIC   Most of us learned to be very critical in our formal education. Finding flaws in arguments, critiquing the fine arts, analyzing historical missteps, and laying out critical arguments in a debate are the gold standards of a rigorous education. When anticipating the future a critical perspective has its place. But temporarily quieting that inner critic can help you suspend judgment and take a more humble approach. Anticipating is an inexact science based more on intuition. To the extent that quieting your inner critic allows you to have a more open mind, it's a good discipline to practice.

Encouraging Divergent Thinking

HIRE PEOPLE WHO ARE DIFFERENT FROM YOU Cognitive psychologists have observed and documented a "similar to me" bias. We tend to like people who are similar and we hire people who are similar. The problem with that is there can be a benefit to working with someone who sees things really differently; diversity, which takes many forms, can help the team generate ideas they might not have otherwise. Some questions to ask as you consider prospective hires: Do team members come from different types of companies—private, public, small, multinational? Do team members represent different disciplines, have different degrees or training, or come from different cultures? Do team members have varied experience outside of the company? We all have expertise and we all have blind spots, but a well-rounded team provides coverage.

ENRICH THE DISCUSSION Find creative ways to dig yourself and your team out of ruts. Read a book that's made the bestseller list, and ask yourselves if any of the concepts apply to your business. Invite guest speakers from other departments or client organizations. Host brown bags and ask experts to share their knowledge and insights. Tour facilities related to your business—visit a store, factory, construction site, or client site to keep your thinking and your discussions fresh. The best path to a solution isn't always the most direct.

EMPOWER PEOPLE TO SPEAK UP A business will be better at anticipating trends if all employees are aware, observant, and willing to speak up. What practices can you put in place to enable people to provide feedback and perspectives in real time? Employees give you hundreds of extra pairs of eyes and ears to sense future potential for your business, and source ideas. And don't forget customers, often the frontline in the realm of possibility. How are you gathering their wisdom and capitalizing on their desires? Make sure that customer feedback is solicited, heard, and responded to. People are more likely to speak up when they know that their ideas will be taken seriously and appreciated. ■

Questions for reflection . . .

What are the two or three things going on in the world that could impact the organization?

Given the current reality, what can I extrapolate from that?

What are the key variables I should consider as I project this into the future?

Whom could I ask for a perspective?

Have I encouraged dialogue and debate?

What is on the horizon?

from the beach.
You can't even
teach someone
else to surf from
the beach."

NAV

Navigate is the process of translating
Strategy and Anticipation into action.
It is real-time, purposeful decision-making,
requiring you to be agile in the moment,
yet always focused on the horizon.
It's leadership's equivalent to surfing.

I first found myself on a surfboard
thanks to my son, Jack. And yet I found
very quickly that the hallmarks of
the sport—focus, balance, and total
commitment—are disciplines I'm
constantly seeking to develop on land. ⇒

IGATE

"If you are about to launch a rocket and that launch trajectory is off by even inches, the rocket is going to be off by miles out in orbit. . . . Mission is what starts that trajectory. Strategy and navigation enables you to stay focused on maintaining that trajectory over time."

JEFF WEINER, *CEO, LinkedIn.com*

Strategy requires course correction; information is never perfect.

When you're surfing, you look back just enough to pick a wave and monitor its progress, then paddle forward to match its speed. Then you feel it take you in a rush, and as you pull yourself up to standing, every muscle of your body calibrates and re-calibrates to the wave's undulating force. Your eyes, meanwhile, are fixed, laser-like, on the horizon. If you look down, you fall. You are completely present and completely committed. Anything less, and the wave swallows you up.

The same is true for a leader. To navigate, you have to choose the opportunities presented in the moment, the "wave" that will bring you that much closer to your goal. You can't allow indecision to become de facto strategy. Once you've chosen, you need to act decisively. Only in action will you discover whether the choice

Keep your body in the present but shift your gaze to the future.

you've made will thrust you onto the beach or wash you out. There's no progress to be made—and in fact, much to lose—by waiting endlessly for a wave to arrive with a neon sign on it, "TAKE THIS ONE." Finally, that forward gaze to the horizon is what it takes to keep the organization forward leaning.

You must be a world-class observer, objectively and continually measuring and interpreting the results of today to make decisions tomorrow. It has been said that one can choose to ignore reality, but one cannot ignore the consequences of ignoring reality. If you hit a barrier that you simply cannot navigate around, you may have to go back to go forward—otherwise you go nowhere.

Something else to remember about Navigate: You can't surf from the beach. You can't even teach someone else to surf from the beach. Although true leaders are masters of delegation, they also need to know when to get their feet wet. There will be critical moments that require you to mind even the smallest details. Pay good attention, and you'll know exactly which they are. ✳

**Plan and think to inform your decision,
but don't procrastinate or second-guess it.**

THINGS TO LISTEN FOR

WHEN THERE **IS** A FOCUS ON NAVIGATE . . .	WHEN THERE **NEEDS** TO BE MORE FOCUS ON NAVIGATE . . .
"Compared to our primary goal, that seems trivial. Let's hold off on it."	"I need you to stop what you're doing and take care of this."
"I'd like to figure out how to get rid of these roadblocks."	"I know it's not a business priority, but this is something I really want to do."
"Some of our underlying assumptions have changed—how do we adjust the plan?"	"I'm not sure what I need to focus on first."

Inaction can be more dangerous than action, and failure to act is a choice.

IDEAS FOR ACTION

Do

Aiming for Your Destination

DEFINE YOUR TARGET The strategy you set for your organization should clearly define your destination. Make sure that everyone shares the same brightly-colored target, so that together you build momentum. Don't fall victim to the "ready-shoot-aim" approach.

MAKE ADJUSTMENTS Think about LinkedIn CEO Jeff Weiner's rocket launch scenario: If a rocket is a fraction of an inch off its trajectory when it launches, it will be miles from its target in orbit. Fortunately, you're running a business, not launching rockets, so you can make adjustments along the way. Aim with precision, but if you are off track, find ways to close the gap between where you are and where you need to be.

The only real failure is failing to fail.

MONITOR YOUR DASHBOARD Pilots constantly make adjustments to their flight plans while in the air, in response to weather and other factors. They have immensely sophisticated navigation tools, as well as air traffic controllers to assist them. Create something similar for your own "flightpath." What's on your dashboard? Who can serve as your air traffic controllers? Think through those questions carefully and make a conscious plan for how often to check your readings.

Staying Focused

PRIORITIZE There is always more to do than resources to do it. Ideas are infinite; bandwidth isn't. Poor prioritization usually means projects start with a bang but end with a whimper, unfinished and forgotten. If you want something to show for your team's time and effort, decide what's most important and stick to it. If you notice your team's focus is wildly out of sync with its priorities, check yourself first. Do you assess whether any given action item is truly important? Do you delegate anything that doesn't require your personal attention? Do you protect your time for strategic priorities? Your ability to squelch distractions and prioritize will set the bar for the entire company.

SAY NO Saying yes to everything is not a strategy. Respect the goals you've defined. When you're at capacity, what falls off the plate? Purposeful decision-making means to evaluate what should stay and what should go, and share them widely. Once you decide that you need to say no to something, consider how to frame it. For example, if it's a valid idea but not within the context of today's focus, clarify that, and make a point to revisit it once goal-related "musts" are handled. You don't want the sharpness of your focus to have a chilling effect on idea generation.

DON'T START THE FIRES Don't just fend off distractions, make sure you're not creating any, either. If you're a good leader, people take your authority seriously—and that means that your offhand suggestion could turn into a full-blown cross-departmental effort, whether or not that was your intention. Stay on message. Ask questions that show people where your focus is. If you see a shiny object to chase, take the time to evaluate whether it merits an amendment to the strategy. Maybe it factors into next year's strategy; maybe it's a total blind alley. Taking the time to reflect before setting things in motion—which is to say, before opening your mouth—will limit the shockwave that reverberates through the entire organization.

Executing

MEASURE AND MONITOR People will focus their efforts on what they know is being measured, so make sure you've got the right metrics defining success. Collect just enough data to provide feedback for course correction and to create small wins and celebrate progress, but not so much that collecting data becomes a competing project. Whenever you can, ask for input about which metrics are most valuable from the employees themselves. At times in my career, I have stopped sending all reports out to business units and employees just to make sure the audience is listening. Data must be meaningful.

USE FEEDBACK Don't ignore feedback. Feedback can come in many forms. It can come from people burning out on your team, from project managers close to the project, from the quality of what's being produced, from initial customer response. Anything that gives an indication of progress is feedback. What you do with it is critical. Some of it may be noise. Some of it may contain invaluable insight that will drive efficiency, productivity, and quality. As a team, analyze and discuss the feedback you are hearing to help figure out what matters, and then respond collaboratively.

MAKE CONTINUOUS IMPROVEMENTS Everything is a work in progress. We do the best we can with the imperfect information that's available. Over time, experience, and especially trial and error, we develop and refine our knowledge. Add new technology to the mix and you've got near constant opportunities to improve process and create more efficient work flows. At regular intervals, take stock of how things are going and what can improve. The improvements you choose to implement may be incremental or they may require a complete overhaul of the system; both approaches can produce meaningful results. Continuous improvement means subscribing to an evolutionary mindset, a commitment to the idea that you can always get just a little bit better—or a lot. ■

Questions for reflection . . .

How can I balance staying the course with being responsive?

If this company accomplishes only one thing this year, what should it be?

How do I evaluate the right focus among myriad ideas and possibilities?

Once I've set the target, how will I track and measure progress?

What sources of feedback will help me understand whether we're on course?

What is a good pace for gathering feedback and making tweaks to continuously improve the process?

"BE KIND, for everyone

is fighting
a great battle."

10

COMMU

When I first became CEO, I was oblivious to a pervasive reality of leadership: You are never *not* communicating. I was so focused on the "message moments" and their content—bold speeches, judiciously worded memos—that I failed to notice that I was still broadcasting the rest of the time, and with the rest of my body.

NICATE

Everything I said and did not say, the words
I chose or avoided, the relative ease of my gait,
where my eyes focused, whether I used this
story or that one, told it in a voice calm or
commanding—there was a message imbued in
each of these tiny moments and the skill with
which I mastered each mattered. It mattered a lot. ⇒

The quality of your communication has a real and profound effect on your company's success. Everything you say or do as a leader makes your people just a little more or a little bit less able to tackle the work before them. You *are* the message, each tiny gesture speaking decibels louder than all the props, the PowerPoints, the graphs, the pie charts. Humans are intuitive, listening first and foremost to your body: They hear what your heart says and know immediately when it conflicts with the words leaving your mouth. Emanating through your physical presence and the sound of your words, how you feel when you communicate—humble, passionate, confident—has the most impact.

Get your heart *and* your head on straight before you speak.

Mastering that heightened self-awareness only gets you halfway there. The rest of the journey toward effective communication relies on your ability to listen and feel—to absorb information even as you're disseminating, and to respond. A leader is a change-maker, not a Roman Senator. You're looking to move people to action. That means your communication needs to be interactive, creating true connection and stirring emotional response.

And so you've got one more big challenge, one we've discussed before: You need to create an environment in which people are comfortable speaking their minds, even or especially when they're talking to the guy who signs their paycheck. Otherwise communication isn't truly interactive; it's not a true two-way street. What you hear is just your own POV reflected back at you, with a worker-bee's smile. Constantly encourage others to share information freely and

Communication is interactive, not a radio broadcast.

to put their authentic self forward, so that all that listening you're doing is time and energy well spent.

Be a model of the authenticity and humility you'd like to see in others. Make these qualities your guiding lights. In *Split-Second Persuasion*, Cambridge psychologist Kevin Dutton relates a story about Winston Churchill meeting with Flight Sergeant James Allen Ward, who had been honored during World War II for climbing onto the wing of his Wellington bomber at 13,000 feet to extinguish a fire in the starboard engine. Ward was completely tongue-tied in Churchill's august presence, and Churchill, noticing this, commented: "You must feel very humble and awkward in my presence." Ward agreed, stammering. "Then you can imagine," continued Churchill, "how humble and awkward I feel in yours." Ward was completely set at ease.

Shift your focus outward to recognize, as Plato did, the need to "be kind, for everyone is fighting a great battle." Climb off your pedestal and honor others, and not only will you communicate more effectively, you'll find your leadership a lot less lonely.

It's not only what you say, it's how you say it.

> "When a leader walks into the room, before he or she speaks the first word, people already have an opinion. . . . Language is an art to express ideas, but energy is what is projected."
>
> PETER GUBER
> *CEO, Mandalay Entertainment*
> *Academy Award-winning producer, businessman, entrepreneur*

Finally, a word about content. Yes, your words matter, too, so pay rapt attention. (There are no breaks here!) As the leader, there's no room for offhand, ill-considered remarks. People will take you literally, so be clear, precise, and constantly aware of the impact of your words. Consider what they'll sound like repeated to others throughout the organization—because they will be repeated!

Communicate strategic intent—yours and the organization's. Share all the facts, but not until you have all the facts. And remember, when you speak, it's on behalf of the entire organization, for others rather than for yourself—"we," "us," and "ours" should be used versus "I," "me," and "my." Whether spoken or written, words or actions, the message must always convey both the leader's vision and the organization's purpose and values. ✺

**Inhale before you exhale,
think before you speak.**

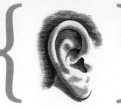

THINGS TO LISTEN FOR

WHEN THERE **IS** A FOCUS ON COMMUNICATE . . .	WHEN THERE **NEEDS** TO BE MORE FOCUS ON COMMUNICATE . . .
"Let's set aside some time to talk this through."	"I didn't actually mean that, I was just thinking out loud."
"Let me be honest with you."	"It seems like lip service. Where are the actions to back it up?"
"Tell me what you think about this."	"I feel like you are talking at me, not with me."
	"Huh?"

Share information freely and be authentic to create a culture that does the same.

IDEAS FOR ACTION

Do

Getting and Keeping Their Attention

TAILOR YOUR MESSAGE   One speech doesn't play across all audiences. Consider who will be listening, then make slight adjustments to the content as well as your tone, pace, and style accordingly. These should be variations on your natural style, not reinventions. Some things to consider: How sophisticated is the audience? What is their context? How spontaneous and participatory are they likely to be? Answering these questions will help you decide what stories to choose; whether to focus on logic or emotion; how best to engage them.

PREPARE   Even if you are a great speaker, it's hubris to think you should ever "wing it." Consider that the strength of your leadership is what's at stake every time you open your mouth. Beyond that, your words are literally valuable—you're paying people for every minute they spend listening. Giving a company-wide speech is a huge investment. Don't waste those words! You cannot over-prepare.

MAKE TACTICAL CHOICES What's your "performance style"? For formal presentations you might stand next to the podium, wander around with a wireless microphone, or mingle in the audience and ask for participation. Which choice plays to your strengths but is also most appropriate to your audience and message? Look for tools or media that will amplify your remarks: video clips, slides, interactive polling, music, lights, interactive webinars, even staged demonstrations to bring your points to life. For ideas, think back to presentations that really moved you and made you think. What facilitated that impact? Leverage those tactics.

Mastering the Art of Written Communication

FIND YOUR VOICE Your words and how you put them together are part of your brand as a leader. You may have a communications or marketing team writing for you. Make sure that you work with them so that they understand your voice and how you want the company and the public to perceive you. Read through quotes and articles being provided to the media. Does the writing sound like you? Does the tone and language reflect who you are in person? Provide the writers with feedback along the way so that they can make appropriate adjustments.

KEEP IT STRAIGHTFORWARD Say what you mean and be clear about it. The best writing in a business context gets the point across efficiently. As the leader, your e-mail will be read, but people are so overwhelmed with information that whether they understand and remember it will depend on how well it's crafted. Consider using headers, bullet points, slogans, and even humor to get the message consumed and digested by as many people as possible. If you feel the need to pontificate, get a pet.

STOP SHORT OF PERFECTION Don't succumb to a never-ending set of drafts and rewrites, wordsmithing a simple e-mail like it's your personal *Leaves of Grass*. Remember the rule of diminishing returns: Once you've hit the 80 percent mark, hit "send." Too much editing can work against authenticity. Everybody has their own style; know yours and resist the impulse of others to edit it out—but only up to the point that it enhances rather than distracts from the message you want to get across.

Communicating Carefully in Difficult Situations

WATCH YOUR MOOD   Take care not to write when you're feeling angry or offended. Deal with your emotions first. Or, if you need to write something out, go ahead—but put it away for 24 hours and then revisit. Rarely is your first, knee-jerk reaction what you really want to communicate. When emotions are high, take a pause.

CONTROL A DIFFICULT AUDIENCE   Some people may want to question your message or your point of view, publicly and perhaps derisively. Above all, stay calm and composed. If they are respectfully engaging you in dialogue, honor their questions and arguments, but don't let them take control of the room. It's a good idea to provide a respectful response in the moment, but don't feel like you have to provide all the answers: "I respect the point you're making and want to honor it with a more in-depth discussion than we can have right now—follow up with me af-

terwards." Don't take too much time with the critic. There are many more people in the audience who want to hear your ideas and ask you questions. You have natural authority as the speaker, and the energy of the room will follow your attention. Respectfully move to more positive interactions.

COMMUNICATING WITHOUT NONVERBALS So much of our communication relies on nonverbal cues. Take special care when your words are divorced from your physical presence. Nuance usually conveyed by tone or expression is often lost in an e-mail. A comment made on a conference call without the benefit of facial cues or hand gestures can be harder to read. When you are managing a remote team or communicating from a distance, pay extra attention to bridging these gaps—and remind others that they exist. Ask for feedback and adjust if necessary. ■

Questions for reflection . . .

Are my words and actions aligned behind the same message?

How do I communicate best? What do I need to work on?

If someone turned off the audio on me, what would they see?

Who is my audience?

Did I think before I spoke?

Do I believe what I'm saying?

"IMAGINE that every

conversation you have is an opportunity to sit at the feet of a guru."

THE ELEVENTH ABSOLUTE
FOR LEADERS:

LISTEN

Businessman Charles O. Rossotti
was celebrated during Bill Clinton's
administration for creating sweeping
change in an organization previously known
mostly for its monolithic intransigence:
the Internal Revenue Service, where he
was commissioner. Rossotti told the business
magazine *Fast Company* the secret of his
success: at first, he didn't change a thing. ⇒

Before anything else, Rossotti wanted to gain the organization's trust. So he spent the first six months meeting with employees across the country. In other words, he did nothing but *listen*. "Too often, people who enter the top echelons of organizations think that they're supposed to know everything," he said. "They think that they've been hired to provide an answer to every question. In fact, people sometimes just want you to listen."

When leaders listen, they aren't just listening to words. They're picking up tone, nuance, and body language; what is said and what is left unsaid. How well you listen determines the quality of the

**The distance between hearing and listening
is thinking and understanding.**

"Talk less and people may assume that you know more."

ALI VELSHI, *Former News Anchor and Chief Business Correspondent,*

CNN; Host, Al Jazeera America

information you gather, but there's another, deeper leadership benefit to doing it right: creating trust.

Trust happens when people understand that not only have you—compassionate, caring you—listened, but that they've been truly heard. And as a leader, you haven't finished the act of listening until you've communicated that back to them.

GE, known for cultivating leadership excellence, has now added "listening" to its list of the most desirable traits in potential leaders. Imagine that every conversation you have is an opportunity to sit at the feet of a guru—or, as executive coach Marshall Goldsmith has suggested, an exploratory first date with the world's most fascinating human. Assume that every exchange is an opportunity to learn something and you'll find that it becomes the case.

Listening takes diligent practice and a singular focus. It may be as foreign to you, and as difficult, as sitting cross-legged for an hour of meditation. It's old school. In the modern, tech-driven world, multitasking may no longer be celebrated as a virtue, but it's still grumpily accepted as a necessary evil.

Don't just listen—show you've listened.

When listening, leaders need to fight that urge with every ounce of their being. Listening is the antithesis of multitasking. You can't simultaneously read a gadget and genuinely engage a human being. Only true presence in the moment will get you to the pinnacle of listening: a shared, unique experience that connects you to the speaker and leaves you both with new perspective. A pause in the rush of business as usual that says, "You matter." Again, in those moments you're developing trust and its twin virtue, loyalty.

But as with "Communicate," a leader's job in listening isn't confined to the moments of exchange. If you want to get the truth out of people, it's up to you to create a track record of being open—which means "open for business" and open to new ideas. Make sure others see you as approachable and ready for candor.

I know one manager, "John," who was looking for a way to protect some of his time for quiet, uninterrupted work. And so he made a bright red stop sign and set it outside his door whenever he needed silence. His intentions were good—but unfortunately his direct reports were offended. Even when he took the sign down, they perceived him as unapproachable. When a leader puts up a barrier of any kind—especially an emergency-red sign, it must be noted—communication breaks down. To be an effective leader means having an open-door policy to listen. Do what it takes to protect that.

Once they're through your door, master a listening style that sets people at ease. Creating pauses by exploring, but not scrutinizing, their words. Ask thoughtful questions and be comfortable with the

Make it safe for others to tell you the truth.

Listening is more than hearing, and it is definitely more than waiting for the other person to take a breath so that you can speak again.

Listen to what you don't want to hear.

silences that follow; don't rush to fill the gaps. If the person doesn't answer right away, wait. Don't jump in to explain, soften the tone, or suggest an answer. Let the person process. Your willingness to pause and listen tells them that the question is important and—even more importantly—her answer is worth waiting for. It takes time and practice, but patient presence in conversation is one of the most effective skills a leader can develop.

Listening is more than hearing, and it is definitely more than waiting for the other person to take a breath so that you can speak again. It is the ability to temporarily forget the future and the past, and collapse your focus to a single point, a single person— here and now. ✳

Listen, learn, and then lead—in that order.

THINGS TO LISTEN FOR

WHEN THERE **IS** A FOCUS ON LISTEN . . .	WHEN THERE **NEEDS** TO BE MORE FOCUS ON LISTEN . . .
"Let me see if I understand what you mean."	"I know what you're going to say."
"Can you say more about that?"	"Excuse me for one minute, let me just take this call."
"I'm interested to hear your perspective on this."	"How can you say that?"

Listening doesn't just give you hard data; it educates your intuition.

IDEAS FOR ACTION

Do

Becoming a More Natural Listener

FIND THE RIGHT MINDSET With listening, humility once again proves to be a core success trait. If you already believe that you know best, then listening becomes a waste of time, and leaders don't waste time. So you hurry to get through any given conversation and check it off your list. Meanwhile, the person senses that immediately and clams up—convenient, since you weren't listening anyway. Check your mindset, because until you're open to the likelihood that you can learn something, you're not going to listen.

MAKE UP FOR YOUR FAULTS Becoming a better listener is like a miracle tonic for some of our most common personality defects. Do people think you're arrogant? Listen more in meetings and that perception will quickly change. Do you intimidate people? Ramp up how much you listen and watch them relax. Hot tempered? Taking time to listen rather than immediately reacting can help you maintain your composure. Listening smoothes so many rough edges.

ADDRESS THE KNOW / DO GAP   You know how to listen just like you know how to eat healthy. And yet there can be a gap between what you know and what you actually do. Until you understand the root cause behind when you choose to listen, whom you choose to listen to, and how attentively you do it, you won't improve. Listening or not listening is a choice you're making in every interaction. Pay attention to your pattern, analyze your choices, and make adjustments.

Focusing on the Fundamentals

BE PATIENT   Work environments are fast-paced. You're busy; you need to maximize efficiency. The question is, at what cost? If you are trying to be efficient by interrupting someone else in the middle of his thought, or finishing his sentence to move things along, you are really telling him that you don't need them. And so, people will stop trying. In the long run, your deaf ear is what's expensive: in lost productivity as the worker disengages, and in who knows what poor decision-making on your part caused by limited information flow.

ASK MORE QUESTIONS   If your goal is to better understand another person's perspective then you'll want to ask a lot of questions. Questions help you clarify and confirm what you've heard. But the type of question matters. Leading questions are really just statements parading around with a question mark; they don't suggest any interest in what's been said or what might be said. If you are truly curious, interested in learning, and willing to explore, your questions will reflect that to others.

WATCH YOUR NON-VERBALS   Are you looking at your watch? Checking your mobile device? Identify distractions and minimize them. Meet with people away from your computer. Leave your phone behind on your desk. Stay focused on making eye contact, taking notes, and asking questions. Every fidget, every glance out the window, every distracted look are felt by your partner in conversation. They could be interpreted as signals that you are bored, disinterested, or that you don't think the exchange is worth your time. Unless those are messages you want to send, build practices that support your desire to give uninterrupted attention. Quite simply, be in the moment.

Listening to Things I Don't Want to Hear

DON'T JUMP TO SOLUTIONS   If you draw conclusions too early in an interaction people will think that you've made up your mind and don't need to hear what they have to say. Leave things open longer than you might be inclined to. Spend extra time exploring the topic from various angles. Ask questions that might help you evaluate different options. Save statements, solutions, and conclusions for the very end of the conversation.

CALMLY FACE THE NEGATIVE   It's much easier to listen to positive feedback than negative. If you find yourself being criticized, acknowledge your discomfort, but set it aside to stay focused in the moment on understanding what the other person is

Listen to educate your intuition.

saying. Don't worry about whether or not you agree with it. As business writer and relationship expert Keith Ferrazzi has written, "It's only data!" Let the people speak their minds; quell your need to react. Ask clarifying questions. Restate what you heard to make sure you understood, and that *they* see that. Only then will they be willing to listen to your response or bring the conversation to a close. Don't feel the pressure to respond in that moment. Thank the other person and assure him that you will spend some time reflecting on what he's said. After you've had time to digest, you can re-engage him in conversation.

COMBAT SELECTIVE LISTENING Everyone has hot buttons, certain issues they don't want to talk about, points of view that they disagree with, topics or people that they find irritating. Practice listening in situations where your modus operandi has been to shut down. Listen for content. Listen objectively without passing judgment. Parse out the points without evaluating them. Find a way to get value from listening to something that you would rather ignore. ■

Questions for reflection . . .

What proportion of the time do I spend listening versus talking?

Am I more focused on what the person is saying or on constructing my next thought or argument?

Do I care what other people think or feel?

Is my office set up to minimize distractions when I'm meeting with someone?

Do I multitask when I'm on a call?

Do I believe that I can learn something new when I'm in a conversation with someone else?

"I HAVE not failed

10,000 times.
I have successfully
found 10,000
ways that will
not work."

THOMAS EDISON

12

THE TWELFTH ABSOLUTE
FOR LEADERS:

LEARN

Business professor and management guru
Gary Hamel says that the most driving
question for today's leaders is, "Are you
learning as fast as the world is changing?"
I've got a ready answer: No. No matter how
smart you are, how adaptable, how agile-
minded, how keen, you're still only one
person who can absorb and process only so
much. The only thing that intellectual or
experiential bona fides really earn you today
is an opportunity to play the game. But to
win, you can't cling to the past, not for
a minute; that's a dead end. ⇒

It's not failure,
it's called learning.

Here's your salvation: You're not a leader because of what you know. You're a leader because you have the wisdom to acknowledge what you *don't know*, and find answers in your most valuable resource—people. In other words, you are always and forever ready to learn from the very people you're charged to lead. The most successful leaders tap the collective intelligence of their entire organizations and co-commit them to the kind of constant reinvention through learning that translates into improving their businesses each and every day.

In *Practical Radical*, William Taylor shares the story of John Fluevog, the celebrity shoe designer who was at first irritated when strangers came up to him again and again in airports, slipping him napkins and sad crumpled scraps with sketches of their ideas for his next genius shoe design. "Who are these amateurs, telling me what to do?" was his reaction. It took years before he finally thought, *these people aren't a nuisance, they're a source of learning.* Shortly thereafter, he built what Taylor calls an "architecture of participation," a means to actively inspire and capture new ideas from his customers. Through the company website, he invited them to send in their design ideas to participate in a contest, with the winning designs manufactured and released by Fluevog, named after their amateur designers. Today, some

**What got you here won't get you there.
Adapt and adopt.**

of the company's best sellers are shoes designed by fans. In Taylor's telling, Fleuvog says the contest was "the most amazing unleashing of energy, creativity, and brainpower that he had ever seen." And all it required was for him to put aside his ego and put a little thought into how to make all those ideas part of his company's agenda.

So, what's your architecture of participation? How can you spur creativity among your people, and then ensure that the ideas don't just rattle around, but are captured and translated into learning and action for everyone else? If you haven't thought hard about these questions, I can guarantee you're tapping only a small percentage of the ever-growing knowledge and experience of your people. If you want to be the kind of person—and build the kind of culture—to whom others rush to share great ideas, you have to develop a persona that attracts them. Actually, here Fluevog is again a solid, if left-field, example—people identified him easily at all those airports because he's a very flamboyant dresser. He *pops*. Without buying a

**Achievements fade; progress inspires
and learning endures.**

"Perspective comes from remembering the past, but not staying there."

MARK THOMPSON, *President and CEO, The New York Times Company*

raspberry beret, how can you become a person who *pops*, whose established persona excites people to learn, act, and share—and in particular, with you?

At Korn/Ferry, we highly value a trait we call "learning agility"—the ability to draw from experience and apply that learning to entirely new situations. In other words, "the learning is the work," as Professor Michael Fullan puts it in his book *The Six Secrets of Change.* Fullan notes that at Toyota, famous for its organizational learning, every manager is a teacher first. Learning happens through performance, as ideas are put to work and either succeed or flounder. "In Toyota's culture, as in all cultures where learning is the work, the trainer is always responsible for the student's success. . . . Learning on the job is explicit, purposeful, and ubiquitous." That attitude needs to permeate every level of your organization, emanating first and foremost from you.

You can help the learning culture along by cultivating in yourself another related trait: unflagging optimism. Everyone likes an

Knowledge breeds confidence; failure lends to wisdom.

optimist; many people, for example, have pointed to optimism as the source of Ronald Reagan's legendary charisma. Optimism will make it easier for you to energize your people around improvement. Built into Taylor's idea of the architecture of participation is the idea that at its foundation, you have to become the kind of person who makes people want to contribute their best and brightest. As the leader, you have to be the one to give energy not consume it. Again, you may not be John Fluevog, but optimism is a great shortcut to his caliber of magnetism.

Optimism is also the outlook you need to encourage and support new endeavors with the full knowledge that a certain percentage of

Continued success requires growth; growth requires learning.

them will fail. "I have not failed 10,000 times," Thomas Edison famously insisted. "I have successfully found 10,000 ways that will not work." That's the outlook you need to empower your people to be willing to learn on the job—and therefore to make mistakes on the job. Earlier I mentioned the need to celebrate and invest in failure to help people think creatively; the real-time learning potential it creates is equally valuable. Mistakes quickly become momentum when we can identify the cause of failure and implement change.

Find ways to "glamorize mistakes," to use Stanford professor Jeffrey Pfeffer's language, so that people are not only brave enough to make them, but brave enough to make them known to others— essential, because otherwise the organization learns nothing. "It may seem counterintuitive," Pfeffer writes in *What Were They Thinking*, "but the most successful people are making many if not more mistakes than most people. The difference is that they don't try to cover them up. They acknowledge them, learn from them and move on."

Again, you as the leader must model the humble, flexible behavior you seek for the rest of the organization. That doesn't always come so easy to many of us hard-charging, Type A people, so make sure to surround yourself with people who will call you on your ego when it flares; who will give you new ideas and shake you from complacency; who will push you to wrench yourself from the day-to-day long enough to spin it around and upside down and see it anew.

As a primary priority, find ways to empower yourself and everyone around you to know, do, and be more—not once a year or when it feels comfortable, but every single day.

Learning never ends. ✳

THINGS TO LISTEN FOR

WHEN THERE **IS** A FOCUS ON LEARN . . .	WHEN THERE **NEEDS** TO BE MORE FOCUS ON LEARN . . .
"I think I see some parallels here."	"I would like a little more predictability and stability here."
"I'm curious to learn more about that."	"That seems risky, I'm not sure we should try it."
"I've never tried that before. Sign me up!"	"I don't even know where to start."

IDEAS FOR ACTION

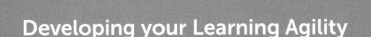

Do

Developing your Learning Agility

ESCAPE YOUR ROUTINE Being on autopilot is the opposite of learning, and it's exactly what your efficient-minded brain does when you're following the same patterns, day after day. Find new and different things to do, places to see, routes to take to work. All of these keep your mind active and alert. Much of learning is being aware and reflecting on yourself, your environment, and your response to the environment. Everyone has a comfort zone, and not much learning happens there. Find the right amount of challenge to keep your mind engaged and learning.

STOP TRYING TO BE PERFECT You may not consider yourself a perfectionist, but most highly successful people have perfectionist tendencies. Think about it: Do you want most people to like you? Do you want to avoid embarrassment? Do you want to avoid taking risks? This is your overactive ego at work, and it

wreaks havoc on your learning agility. Get comfortable with acting even when you don't have all the information. Get used to
the idea that pursuing new ideas involves risk. And recognize
that the only way to get through life without being criticized is
to never leave your house. Get ready to make mistakes and even
to take flack for them.

TACKLE A PROBLEM   People who are learning agile are quintes-
sential problem solvers. You give them a tough problem that stumps
everyone else and they will come up with three viable solutions.
They probably don't do it all on their own—they are resourceful,
too. This is a skill that you can practice: Find a new problem to
tackle and have at it. Look at it from every angle. Ask other people
how they would approach it. Think of analogies that might shed
light on a solution. Be relentless. Persevere.

TIGHTEN YOUR PROCESS Make sure that you understand and
can operationalize what's working in your organization today.
By getting the ship running smoothly, you are freeing up energy
for working on innovative practices that get even greater results.

Developing Your Leadership Skills

BUILD SELF-AWARENESS   Know your strengths and weaknesses. Be an expert when it comes to *you*. Consider doing some

sort of skills audit. It could be a self-assessment, or even better, a multi-rater assessment. Once you've polled people, take stock of the feedback. Work with a coach or a mentor to reflect on the themes that you're noticing. Self-awareness is an incredible antidote for an outsized ego.

BUILD A DEVELOPMENT PLAN   Based on your current leadership skill profile and what's important for success, determine what is important to fix and what you can leave alone. It all depends on what's mission critical for your current role and your future aspirations. Build a development plan and find someone who can keep you accountable to taking the actions and checking on progress.

SEEK REGULAR FEEDBACK   It's difficult to get honest feedback when you're at the top. People may feel intimidated by you, or they may worry about repercussions if they give you constructive feedback. That's why it's important for you to take the initiative. Find people you trust, who will be honest with you no matter what. Ask these people if it's okay for you to seek their feedback on occasion. Once they know that you are serious, you will begin hearing very valuable feedback that can shape your leadership of the organization.

The more you experiment, the more you learn.

Being Adaptable

STAY ON YOUR TOES When athletes stay on their toes they are equally poised to move in any direction, ready to quickly adapt and respond. In this case, staying on your toes means not becoming attached to any one solution. Be committed to trying different things and learning along the way. This way you'll pivot quickly in light of new revelations.

TRY RAPID PROTOTYPING Quick experiments require less investment and commitment but give you room to fail. Many creative ideas never make it to market. The innovations that do make it to the market also have a low success rate. The most successful innovators try a lot of quick, inexpensive experiments to increase the chances of success. The more you experiment, the more you learn.

REVERSE IT Take a stubborn problem and turn it inside out. Artists pay careful attention to the "negative space." Define what the problem is *not*, what's missing from the problem, or what the mirror image of the problem is. Turning the problem upside down can often bring fresh perspective that leads to breakthrough thinking. ■

Questions for reflection . . .

What are some key experiences that have impacted my leadership? What did I learn from those experiences?

How do I approach challenges that I have never encountered before?

When was the last time I was a beginner at something?

Do I acknowledge when I don't know something?

What are some things that I would like to learn more about?

EPILOGUE

IT'S ALL ABOUT THE PEOPLE

I've mentioned before that leadership can be lonely. "Uneasy is the head that wears the crown," moaned a sleepless Henry IV. And it is true that as a leader, always thinking and acting with both the organization's and your employees' well-being in mind, you experience a certain remove. Total accountability does that.

And yet, twenty-first-century leadership, now more than ever, is not unilateral; it requires others. That is the pervasive theme of this book, and the key insight to lightening your burden. Despite all of the technological innovations of the last century, it is people that make businesses successful. Yes, a leader needs to know how, what, when, and why, but in the end, a leader is in the people business. The reality is that you're not doing it alone, and the more you connect emotionally and authentically with your colleagues, the more you find ways to make them leaders in their own spheres, the less you will mistake leadership for a lonely throne.

Elevate your colleagues—yes, they are your *colleagues*, if not your peers—closer to your level by defining a common purpose—the "why"—that inspires them to invest themselves in their work as much as you do because doing so satisfies their own hopes and dreams. Empower them to make decisions that matter, and to enjoy, and occasionally endure, the consequences of independent thought.

As the leader, if you are looking for people to believe in you, you will be waiting for results—rather, believe in people, and you will be amazed by the results.

In the digital age, change happens at the speed of electrons. The paradox, however, is that there's only one way to keep up: by relying on things that should not change—the values and the qualities of leadership that are absolute. ☀

Success must breed humbleness, failure must impart wisdom.

ACKNOWLEDGMENTS

I wish to express my deepest appreciation to all of those who supported in the development of Lead.

To my Korn/Ferry colleagues for changing many lives in the world, including my own.

I also wish to acknowledge our team, including Mike Distefano, Dan Gugler, Evelyn Orr, Roland Madrid, Robert Ross, Dana Martin Polk, Tricia Crisafulli, and Tahl Raz.

A special thanks to our publisher, John Wiley & Sons, and our editor Lauren Murphy, Adrianna Johnson, Deborah Schindlar, and their team, for their professionalism, enthusiasm, and commitment to this project.

And to the anchors in my life, who inspired many of the words you will read and remind me daily that it is not what I do, but who I am that matters: my wife, Leslie, and my children, Allison, Emily, Jack, Olivia, and Stephanie.

CREDITS

Illustrations

Kent Barton
Chapter 4; pages 60–61, 63, 65
Chapter 8; pages 124–125, 126, 129
Chapter 12; pages 184, 187, 189

Marty Blake
Chapter 1; pages 8, 13, 19
Chapter 5; pages 77, 78, 81
Chapter 9; pages 141, 143, 144

Chris Gall
Introduction; page 2
Chapter 3; pages 43, 45, 46
Chapter 7; pages 109, 111
Chapter 11; pages 169, 170, 173

Bruce Hutchison
Chapter 2; pages 26–27, 28, 30
Chapter 6; pages 94–95, 96
Chapter 10; pages 154–155, 157, 163
Epilogue; page 201

Design by Ross/Madrid Group, Inc., Los Angeles, California

If you care about the success
of a colleague or friend,
give them this book.